In the
Shadow
of the
Rising Sun

An aerial view of Changi Gaol, Singapore
Archives and Oral History Dept., Singapore

In the Shadow of the Rising Sun

Mary Thomas

Marshall Cavendish
Editions

© 2009 Mary Thomas
First published in 1983
This edition published by Marshall Cavendish Editions
An imprint of Marshall Cavendish International
1 New Industrial Road, Singapore 536196

Cover images: Mary doing her work in an open field in the late 1950s and postcards sent to her during her internment in Changi Prison.

The author donated her Changi artwork and documents to the Imperial War Museum in London. Some of these are reproduced in this book with the kind assistance of the museum.

Other Marshall Cavendish Offices:
Marshall Cavendish Ltd. 5th Floor, 32-38 Saffron Hill, London EC1N 8 FH, UK
• Marshall Cavendish Corporation. 99 White Plains Road, Tarrytown NY 10591-9001, USA
• Marshall Cavendish International (Thailand) Co Ltd. 253 Asoke, 12th Flr, Sukhumvit 21 Road, Klongtoey Nua, Wattana, Bangkok 10110, Thailand • Marshall Cavendish (Malaysia) Sdn Bhd, Times Subang, Lot 46, Subang Hi-Tech Industrial Park, Batu Tiga, 40000 Shah Alam, Selangor Darul Ehsan, Malaysia

Marshall Cavendish is a trademark of Times Publishing Limited

National Library Board (Singapore) Cataloguing in Publication Data
Thomas, Mary, 1906-
In the shadow of the rising sun / by Mary Thomas. – Singapore : Marshall Cavendish Editions, 2009.
p. cm.
ISBN-13 : 978-981-261-859-7

1. Thomas, Mary, 1906- 2. World War, 1939-1945 – Personal narratives, English.
3. World War, 1939-1945 – Prisoners and prisons, Japanese. 4. Prisoners of war –
Singapore – Biography. 5. Prisoners of war – England – Biography. I. Title.

D805
940.548142 – dc22   OCN298772500

Printed by Utopia Press Pte Ltd

To the Memory of

Rev. A.C. Parr, died in a P.O.W. Camp
in Thailand of dysentery and malaria,
June 1943,
aged 39 years

Evelyn Parr, his wife, died in internment
in Sumatra of dysentery and beri-beri,
January 1945,
aged 39 years

My youngest brother, Lt. Christopher Thomas,
killed in action in Burma,
27 January 1944,
aged 25 years

Remembering also:

My brother, Francis, Prisoner of War
in Changi, Thailand and Japan (1942–1945);
Minister of Communications and Works
in Singapore's first independent Government, 1955–1958;
Headmaster of St. Andrew's School, 1963–1973;
died of cancer in Singapore, 12 October 1977,
aged 65 years

Mercy and truth are met together (Psalm 85, v.10)

In Changi Gaol

Bright in the yards, where night descends
The floodlight lamps put out the stars:
The indoor lights on prison walls
Cast shadows of the prison bars.

In one short hour the lights go out:
All sounds grow silent one by one.
Then shine the re-awakened stars
And all the prison world is gone.

Contents

1 Prologue: Before the War

The six years I spent in Singapore, from 1939 to 1945, were not my first experience of life abroad or in the Far East. I was born in December 1906, the eldest of six children of the rector of a small village in the Cotswold hills in Gloucestershire, the other five all being boys. As we grew older we were sent to boarding schools and when I was eighteen I went to St. Anne's College, Oxford, and took a degree in the Honours School of Modern History. The next two years I spent in British Columbia where an aunt, who was also my godmother, was married and living in Vancouver Island. While I was there, I did some teaching.

I decided not to settle in Canada and in order to see more of the world I returned to Great Britain via the Pacific, staying for ten days with friends in Hong Kong, and spending five months with my eldest brother who was manager of a tea estate in Ceylon. I also spend six weeks with friends in Chittagong in Bengal. There had recently been much unrest in Chittagong, and my host had formed the habit of driving to his office with his revolver ready on his knee, for fear of an ambush, but when I was there things were quiet. My hostess was friendly with some Indian families, and I went with her to an

Indian Women's Club and to tea with an Indian businessman and his wife. For such activities she was ostracised by most of the members of the English Club, and when she gave a tea party during my visit for some Indian ladies and their children, only one other Englishwoman would come.

I loved both Indian and Ceylon, partly for their strangeness and the fact that they were so different from anything I had previously known, and partly for their beauty. From my brother's bungalow in Ceylon, one looked across the slopes of the tea plantation with its shady trees to distant mountains which I can see in my mind's eye still. In Chittagong the huge flowering trees and the brilliant colouring everywhere were a never-failing source of delight. I liked, too, the quiet, unhurried pace of life in both countries, where "now" seemed to stretch both forward and backward everlastingly.

When I reached England again, I had another period of teaching but I never felt at home in this work, and after taking a secretarial course I became a secretary at the Cotswold Equitation School at Burford in Oxfordshire, six miles from my village home. I enjoyed this very much as I learnt to ride and could sometimes help with the horses, but on the outbreak of war with Germany, the School closed down.

I tried to join the British Nursing Service as a volunteer auxiliary, known since World War I as the V.A.D. but there was a waiting list of 20,000. I then applied to join the Women's Land Army but there was a waiting list of 8,000. As all the women's services were in much the same state I was advised to stay quietly at home until someone happened to want me. This was a depressing prospect, and at the suggestion of my brother Francis, who was on leave from Singapore where he was an assistant master at St. Andrew's School, I returned there with him.

We landed in Singapore early in the morning in December 1939. The ugly, unimpressive waterfront was bathed in the peaceful light of early day—light with a peculiar quality of softness and freshness like a radiant June morning in England, with no promise of the glare and heat to follow. The big, sprawling city was still asleep, quite quiet and empty. We took a taxi and drove from the docks through the slum areas of Chinatown, then through a few streets of commercial buildings, offices of English firms, and finally along Serangoon Road, a long road of native shops coloured white, bright blue or sea-green, interspersed with Eurasian and Asian bungalows, till we reached the site of the new St. Andrew's School.

This was an old rubber estate, about three miles from Raffles Place, the business centre of Singapore. The new buildings were nearly completed when we arrived and were brought into use a few months later, the school moving out from the rather ramshackle quarters it had previously occupied in the city. The district had been officially scheduled for factory buildings and there were many open stretches of country round about.

The new school buildings stood at the top of a small area of rising ground, with a view over a narrow river, some groves of rubber trees and two large disused gravel pits full of water, which looked like ornamental lakes. A little mist still hung over them, through which distant casuarina trees showed faintly, while the heavy dew which soaked the grass sparkled intermittently where the sun caught it and lay blue and cold in the shadows. Huge, beautiful trees, "jungle trees" of different kinds, were still dotted over the little hill. They were tall and mostly rather bare, showing the odd shapes and twists of their trunks and branches. Some were festooned with ferns while others were streaked with masses of purple flowers. The school architect had wanted to cut down all these lovely trees, and the headmaster and his wife had had a great fight to prevent him. Among them was a small tree called *Bunga Manis*, Sweet Flowers, with white blossoms like jasmine. Its scent used to drift on the wind to the verandah where we sat in the evening.

Singapore lies at the extreme tip of the Malayan peninsula, only about two degrees north of the equator. Its climate is therefore fully tropical and as it lies low, it is also very damp. This tremendous humid heat, though not necessarily unhealthy, is exceedingly trying. The seasons scarcely vary and are little affected by the changes of the monsoon. Generally, stormy weather can be expected in February and March, the greatest heat in May, June and July, while the climate is least oppressive from October to January. It is seldom cool except sometimes at night or when it rains all day occasionally. Storms are frequent and are mostly very violent and fairly brief, with a tremendous downpour of rain and a fierce accompanying gale. They are usually sudden and sometimes travel so quickly that there is only half a minute's warning before the rain descends in a soaking downpour, which may last from ten minutes to four hours.

The great heat affected some people more than others, but nearly everyone tended to become anaemic, and was prone to chills and severe colds from draughts. On the hottest days, the sweat poured off one on the least exertion or even while sitting still. Though this climate need not be detrimental to health, it is extremely enervating to Europeans. Malaria was under very good control but dengue fever was fairly common. Sunstroke was uncommon and it was unnecessary to wear a hat unless one was going to be out in the sun for hours on end. I never wore one except when sailing on Sunday mornings. The glare was tremendous, and out of doors I wore the darkest glasses I could buy. The climate of Singapore is unlike that of Malaya where the monsoon changes are definitely marked, and where the nights, inland at any rate, are much cooler. The white brilliance of the moonlight of a tropic night must be seen to be believed. It blanches the black roads, overlaying them as it were, with a ghostly film of whiteness while the shadows are clear-cut and impenetrable. The colours of leaves and flowers, though soft and subdued, are deep and vivid.

A few days before my brother and I arrived, the Headmaster, the Rev. R. K. S. Adams, and his wife had left for their Christmas holiday at the Government hill station. They had offered us the use of their house and put us up for some months. Later, the second master, the Rev. Cecil Parr, went on leave to England and we occupied his house until he returned, this time with a wife. By then the tall, old-fashioned wooden bungalow for my brother had been cleared for our occupation and we moved in.

On the day that I arrived, I was introduced to what were considered the basic essentials of feminine life in the tropics—the matter of servants and the social life of clubs. My brother had a servant, a Chinese "Boy" called Cheng Ah Moy who had been with him for nearly five years. He was presented to me, greeting my arrival with the distinctly modified rapture which was the usual reaction of oriental servants to the coming of a woman into a bachelor household.

Ah Moy's wife had had a temporary mental breakdown during my brother's absence and had tried to knife the wife of Mr. Adam's Malay syce (chauffeur). He had been told that he must find other quarters for her, and had accordingly obtained a room for her and his two sickly children two miles away and was anxious to return to work for my brother, while going home to his family every night. This was an unusual arrangement as servants always lived with their families on the premises. However, my brother agreed to it, having a sort of affection for Ah Moy, a man of character and capacity. He was devoted to his family, very honest and loyal to us and able to do any sort of work from rearing chickens to cooking, mending, driving and repairing the car.

He was an elderly, rather nervous person, fond of solitude. The other school servants considered him to be *sombong* (stuck-up), but he was not quarrelsome. At the Chinese Festival of Lanterns in 1941, I was travelling along Serangoon Road in the bus when I saw a shop full of attractive paper lanterns. I got off and bought a large one which cost a dollar. It was a splendid specimen, shaped like a pagoda and hung with bits of coloured paper, little bells and pieces of glittering glass which swung and tinkled from its corners in the most delightful fashion. It was impossible to get onto the bus with it as it would certainly have been crushed in the crowd so I walked the two miles home, wondering what I was to do with it. I solved the difficulty by presenting it to Ah Moy for his children. His eyes nearly popped out of his head.

"Oh, Missy!" he said. "Oh, Missy!" His pleasure was too great for other words. While I was having tea he came to speak to me.

"That lantern, it was very expensive?" he asked. "Missy had paid a great deal for it?" To have such a fine lantern to hang outside his room during the Festival meant something very special to him.

St. Andrew's was a Mission School and the normal European feeling against Asians and Eurasians was not current among its staff. Schoolboys and old boys constantly came in to see my brother. I met local-born members of the school staff, visited them occasionally and was entertained at the New World entertainment park by a party of Chinese before I had been in the country a week. I also contrived the costumes for a school production of "The Rivals", which entailed much unaccompanied shopping for cheap materials in Arab Street where, (according to an Englishwoman whom I met at a club) "*No white woman could safely go alone!*" I also grasped the significance of my position as an Englishwoman so little that, unaware that I was doing anything unusual, I treated the other secretary in the commercial office where I worked for a time just as I would anyone else, although she was Eurasian.

In the evening, I sometimes went for a walk in the neighbourhood of the school. There were some open stretches of rough grass. There were two huge cemeteries, one Chinese, the other Muslim, both pleasant places where one could stroll and forget one was living in a large commercial city. There were also the Alkaff Gardens, laid out in Chinese style by the Alkaff brothers, wealthy Arabs who had made fortunes in Singapore and had presented these gardens to the public. They were small but very quiet and pretty, planted with flowering shrubs and casuarinas. They had two little artificial hills and a lake crossed by a red wooden hump-backed bridge, shaded here and there by weeping willows and other ornamental trees.

This life was not at all characteristic of that of most Englishwomen in the East. The majority of them were married and had no job, and few Englishmen or women ever had any social contact with either Asians or Eurasians on any equal terms. Life centred round clubs, cinemas, golf courses and hotels, and most clubs would not allow non-Europeans on the premises even as guests. On the whole, Englishwomen in the East led easy lives. Their domestic responsibility was close to none in a country overflowing with capable servants. Most households had at least three servants, an amah, a cook-houseboy and a syce, and often there were more. People filled up their time with bridge, shopping, coffee-drinking with friends in the morning and resting on their beds all afternoon. In the evening, there was the club, dancing and the cinema. Everybody had a car and my travelling to work by bus was regarded as something rather strange and not quite suitable.

My brother and I belonged to one club only, the Yacht Club. The members had a common keen interest in sailing, which gave it a happier and homelier atmosphere than that of most clubs. After learning to sail by crewing in other people's boats, I bought a dinghy and became a yachtswoman, surviving several capsizals, and happy in the peace, space and solitude of the wide harbour waters. Real sailing, not racketing about with an outboard motor or other engine, must surely be one of the most heavenly recreations life affords.

Europeans took local leave at the two Malayan hill stations, Cameron Highlands and Fraser's Hill. Cameron Highlands, about six thousand feet up, was a newly developed resort with several hotels, a rest house, a golf course, and many bungalows belonging to various firms where their European employees could take holidays. It also had two schools for European children. My brother, two friends, a young married couple and I took a bungalow for a four-week holiday at Ringlet, a village about six miles from Cameron Highlands proper and about a thousand feet lower. We spent our time going for long tramps through the jungle and over the tea plantations, with occasional excursions to a hotel for a proper meal when we got tired of feeding ourselves out of tins. It was a pleasant four weeks, much more like a summer holiday in the Canadian backwoods than a holiday in the East. We had a Malay servant called Bujang, who spent most of his time gambling in the local café. He used to fetch our provisions for us, but otherwise confined his labours to cleaning our muddy shoes. We did everything else ourselves, and though I sometimes thought it would be rather nice, on coming back at 3 p.m. from a four-hour ramble, to find a meal ready instead of having to get it ourselves, this simple life was in fact a pleasant change.

When I was teaching, I had the usual school holidays, and the summer before the war broke out I spent three weeks at Fraser's Hill, an older hill station run by the Government primarily for government servants. This was a charming place. I stayed in the rest house and went for endless long walks along the jungle trails which were kept cleared for the benefit of visitors, though not many appeared to take advantage of them. The jungle has a fascination of its own. It is very cool and extraordinarily peaceful. After walking for a while, you get very hot and sweaty, but the jungle at Fraser's Hill never seemed oppressively close. All sorts of unfamiliar plants grow there, from a blue phosphorescent fern hidden close under dark banks to a spreading creeper something like honey-suckle, which splashes its flame-coloured flowers over the trees in great mats and curtains. Seen from outside these glow brilliantly for long distances against the packed foliage.

In a jungle-covered landscape, dead trees stand out bleached white against the prevailing green, and often on top of a hill, so smooth and blue in the distance that one would think it were covered with turf instead of with impenetrable forest, one tree sticks up solitary against the sky. The trouble with the jungle is that except where paths have been deliberately planned and cut, there is very rarely a view. You are enclosed in greenness and growing things, with only glimpses of sky overhead to remind you that this is not all that exists in the world. I did not see any tigers, leopards and such wild creatures, and people who knew the jungles said that the animals were very timid and mostly preferred to keep out of the way. There were a few birds, brilliant butterflies and some insects, mostly ants and millipedes. In some places there were also wah-wah monkeys, swinging about in the treetops and calling to each other across the valleys. They had a very full, sweet cry, grieving and plaintive, like a baby talking to itself but stronger and clearer and with less variety. The same sweet, sorrowful sounds were repeated over and over again. I scarcely met anyone on these walks. After the crowds and the sophistication of Singapore, the solitude, the indifference and the beauty of the jungle were like a spell, promising and almost giving something that life never does quite give. I think my happiest hours in Malaya were spent wandering alone in the jungle.

Such were Malaya and Singapore as I saw them during the two years between 1939 when I landed, and December 1941, when the first bombs fell. Singapore was typical of all the large towns in Malaya. It is difficult to convey to people who have never been to the East the atmosphere of the easy life of the Europeans in those days. The unchallenged prestige of a ruling and privileged race was automatically the right of almost every white person. Salaries by comparison with those in England were high, the cost of goods and services were low, and the standard of living and comfort which was considered essential for Europeans was quite luxuriously high compared with what we would all have been content with at home. Except for a few professional women, doctors, nurses and teachers, hardly any woman ever did any work which could conceivably be delegated to a paid employee.

During that period, the war in Europe seemed to have little or no repercussion on our lives. Social and club life went on as usual, only a little interrupted when the younger men were called up for two months' military training with the Volunteers. It was not necessary to ration any commodity. Food, imported or native-grown, tinned, frozen or fresh, was plentiful, and so were clothing materials. There were a few little trials: it was difficult to get spare parts for English-made cars, there was a serious shortage of hairpins, and when one was having a new dress made, it was sometimes impossible to get buttons to match. There was no need for black-out or curfew and no one took Air Raid Precautions (A.R.P.) very seriously, for we knew that Singapore was an impregnable fortress. The Japanese, however they might flourish in China, would certainly crumple up the moment they came in contact with a first-class Western power. Presumably the Malayan government was concentrating on keeping England supplied with rubber and tin, both very necessary.

There were not enough aeroplanes, anti-aircraft guns and extra troops trained in tropical warfare to defend England, let alone to spare them for distant Asia. Few of us in Malaya seemed to realise this. The soldiers whom I met appeared as confident and carefree regarding the future as the civilians. I knew only an officer, a man on special service from India, who had taken the trouble to learn Malay. Others who had been quartered three years in the country could not speak one word of it. They could not give the simplest order or ask the simplest question in the widely spoken language of the country. Apparently they had never visualised their duties taking them anywhere out of reach of the educated natives of the towns, where they could get someone to interpret for them.

During this period Singapore was shocked and somewhat amused by the revelations of the Loveday scandal. Captain Loveday was the officer in charge of all the business arrangements with building and allied firms in Malaya for putting up constructions required by the army, from huts for coolies to concrete gun emplacements. Very little business was done in the East without a few palms being greased in the process, but Captain Loveday went so far that, at the instigation of the Civil Police, an enquiry was instituted and a trial held. The General insisted that this should be fully public. It was reported in detail in all the newspapers. Captain Loveday had organised the various firms into a ring and no firm which was not a member had any hope of any army contract. The details of these contracts were settled at meetings between Loveday and the various parties. On these occasions, he was often accompanied by his wife carrying a knitting bag, into which she would stuff the little douceurs of up to $30,000 at a time.

He was estimated to have accumulated between two and three hundred thousand dollars at least. The work, for which the government was in any case paying quite fantastic prices, was often carried out in the most slovenly and inadequate manner. The most shocking instance concerned gun emplacements along the coast, of which concrete was already crumbling before the war with Japan had broken out. Captain Loveday received a sentence of two years' imprisonment, most of which he served as an internee. Shortly after his sentence was passed, the defaulting Chinese cashier of a European firm, who had embezzled about $30,000 of his employers' money, received a sentence of seven years' imprisonment.

War work went on during these two years. Ladies made bandages, woollen scarves, operation stockings, helmets, gloves and pullovers. There were funds for buying bombers and many shops had war aid collecting boxes on their counters marked *Tolong sedikit*—Help a little. A.R.P. began to be organised and there were appeals from the various organisations which required members, notably the Medical Auxiliary Service. I joined as a V.A.D., voluntarily signing a promise that I would continue my work whatever circumstances might arise. Leisured women could get very complete and efficient training as V.A.Ds, but I was working every day and I could not get to the classes very often.

As the threat from Japan came close, we began to have occasional black-out practices, and the advisability of putting white traffic lines down the centre of the main city roads in case of a permanent black-out was considered. Slit trenches were dug, blast-proof walls erected, and the members of the Army Volunteer Corps received two months' military training in a camp. The Governor, Sir Shenton Thomas, announced that with regard to evacuation of civilians in case of an invasion, no distinction whatever would be made between Europeans and others, an order which in practice was variously interpreted by individual subordinates. The tone of the newspapers and of public feeling generally remained quiet and confident, and the tenor of life was still more or less unchanged.

Looking back it seems impossible to believe that anyone in the country had any idea of the strength of Japan or of our own weakness. If they had, they kept very quiet about it. We were strong in the confidence of our own propaganda. We had the naval base, so widely advertised, and magnificent airfields. It troubled nobody, perhaps nobody knew, that there were scarcely any aeroplanes and at the most about six big anti-aircraft batteries in the whole of Malaya. We knew we had soldiers who had spent years in Malaya, and more were coming, and the fact that hardly any of them had ever set foot in the jungle worried nobody. The jungle was in no one's thoughts: it might not have existed except on paper, and was well known to be impenetrable. Thus, in spite of a conviction that war was certainly coming, and in spite of the very serious straits for men and equipment at home of which we knew, our attitude in Malaya remained casual and light-hearted. Ours was an impregnable fortress which could only be attacked from the sea, and proper arrangements had been made to deal with that by means of splendid batteries, innumerable gun emplacements, and quantities of barbed wire in the sea itself and along all the coastal roads. Nothing had prepared us in the slightest degree for the sort of thing which actually lay ahead.

Birthday Ode

For Jill Dawson, Changi Prison, 1942

Ring out, wild bell, to the wild sky
For Jill was born today!
Strike the bell harder, Mrs. White,
Nor care what people say!

O Cell, today do not sweat dust!
Ye Cockroaches, retire!
And yield, ye warring Internees,
Who block the only fire!

Far hence, Profane! (We mean the Foe.)
Today do not defile
With martial, flat, officious feet
A-IV's exclusive aisle.

Ah, when she used to celebrate
With theatres, cakes and ale,
She little thought she'd ever keep
Her natal feast in jail.

About her cell her loving friends
Will gather very soon,
And one may bring some coconut,
Another bring a prune.

And one a priceless cigarette,
And one a useful purse
Looted long since, and empty now:
And I shall bring this verse.

Ah, mourn not those departed days,
The feasting, fun and wealth:
Tonight beneath the twinkling stars
We meet and drink her health.

And when in nineteen-forty-three
Comes twenty-seven September,
And healths are drunk in bright champagne,
This birthday she'll remember.

2 When the Bombs Fell

The first bombs fell on Singapore at about 4 o'clock in the morning of 8 December 1941, doing a little damage in the European shops in Raffles Place but causing most damage and hundreds of casualties in the crowded slums of the dockside and harbour areas. The city was unwarned. It was lit up as usual, a fact which gave rise later to rumours about treachery and carelessness in our own forces. It was strange that there should have been no general warning. A woman friend who was staying with friends near the Singapore General Hospital told me that they were wakened at about 1 a.m. by a telephone call from a personal friend in the Police. He told them that news had just been received that Japanese raiders were on their way. The household got up, the women dressed themselves in slacks, and everyone took down curtains and rolled up carpets in case of fire breaking out. When the bombs fell, this household was awake, alert and perfectly prepared. They were astonished next day to find that the warning had not been general, and that the rest of the world had been caught asleep in their beds by the bombs.

Immediately after this there was a call-up of all members of the Auxiliary Forces to their posts. I became an Assistant Superintendent at St. Andrew's School Aid Post. I was in charge of a shift of some ten Asian and Eurasian nurses, a few of them trained from St. Andrew's Mission Hospital, the rest rather more untrained than I was. The Japanese were intent on taking the city in as undamaged a state as possible, and as ours was not an area of any military importance we never had any bombs within a mile of us and consequently no casualties worth speaking of, though people who had been caught in raids in town came to us daily from their homes for minor dressings. We were used as a depot for the refugees from Malaya who soon began pouring into Singapore by every train and every boat, by lorry and by car.

The head of the Aid Post was Padre Adams. Under him were: Mr. Dong, a Chinese schoolmaster in charge of the ambulance men, and Sister Simpson in charge of the nursing staff. They worked in three shifts under the direction, respectively, of Mrs. Parr who was a masseuse by profession and a trained V.A.D.; Miss Angus, the Eurasian matron of the school; and myself. Mr. and Mrs. Kiong ran the canteen. Most of the local-born members of the Aid Post staff were in some way connected with the school and knew Padre and Mrs. Adams well, and they all showed great loyalty and devotion to their jobs.

Mrs. Adams, who had done excellent work catering for our large and shifting numbers, was pregnant and therefore left by plane for Australia at the end of January. Her friend, Mrs. Allgrove, carried on in her place until 11 February, when she too left. Her husband was in the Volunteers. As they had three children in Australia, she felt she should be with them in case of his being killed. The ship she sailed on was twice attacked, and she was first wounded and then drowned when the ship was sunk. My brother and Mr. Parr had both been mobilised in the Volunteers, Mr. Parr as an army chaplain and my brother in the Bomb Disposal Corps, so they were not working at the Aid Post. After the fall of Penang, the organisation of all the medical work at the Post was in the hands of a Penang evacuee, Dr. Gunstansen. He was efficient, cheerful, practical and courageous. When our wounded had to be evacuated from the Johore coast, a difficult and responsible job, he was specially sent to help.

The work of the school had stopped, and many of the classrooms were turned into hospital wards for wounded English soldiers. This was separate from the Aid Post and had its own medical staff and a nursing staff consisting of European district nurses from Malaya who had been evacuated before the Japanese advance. The matron in charge of the hospital was a great busybody and spent her evenings going round the school buildings with a torch, trying to catch the off-duty nurses, (the Aid Post staff, not her own) who were flirting in corners or sitting out in cars with the fire fighters and ambulance men. She worried Mr. Adams about these matters till his hair turned several shades greyer.

One evening, when he had managed to hide from her, she burst into the casualty room where I was working and tried to order me to go and interfere too. As it happened, we were dealing with the first real casualty to be brought in while I was on duty—a drunken Tamil who had fallen off his bicycle in the black-out and had injured a leg in a drain. He had been brought to the Aid Post for attention and was fighting mad. He had already bitten the doctor in the hand and broken his stethoscope, and was now lying on the treatment table, more or less quiescent after a shot of morphine. A casualty was nothing to matron compared with the inequities of a petting party. She was most indignant when I explained that I could not join her. A few weeks later I consulted her as to what the European nursing staff ought to do in the event of the Japanese capturing Singapore. Should we stay and carry on with our work or go while we could? Was it likely that European women would be liable to worse treatment than the local-born? Matron was over sixty. She drew herself up proudly as I put my question.

"Miss Thomas," she said, "I do not know what will happen to us if the Japanese take Singapore. I don't think they ever will. But, if they should, whatever they may compel us to do we will do it proudly in our country's service!" I bowed my head in assent and went away, wondering if Matron would be asked to do much by even the most licentious Japanese. But as it turned out she left on Friday 13, before capitulation, and was killed with many others when the ship she sailed in was sunk.

Singapore meanwhile was being bombed fairly constantly, mostly in the military and waterfront areas. The chief sufferers were the poorer classes who lived in the adjacent slums though some bombs, in the neighbourhood of the Airport for example, also fell upon the houses of the well-to-do and in the European residential area. The Government House was also bombed. The night raids were mostly planned to take advantage of the bright moonlight, and on such nights we were often disturbed, sometimes two or three times in one night. There were also numerous daylight raids. In the neighbourhood of the Aid Post, our chief danger was from falling pieces of shell from a big anti-aircraft gun about a mile away. The recoil of its discharge shook the whole school in a terrifying manner every time it was fired.

As the Japanese advance drew nearer, more and more Europeans and some Asians left the city. In theory, all members of the Auxiliary Forces, Fire Fighters and Medical Services were supposed to stay until they had orders to go, but actually the principle of *sauve-qui-peut* became more and more the order of the day. People would be on duty one day and the next they would have vanished, leaving no word behind and without making arrangements of any kind for the continuance of their work. When people in senior, responsible posts did this, it was very difficult for subordinates to carry on, or to know what they should do.

Some people maintained that it was the duty of the Europeans to get away and declared that orders should have been given to that effect. Others thought that they would be more useful elsewhere than as prisoners in the event of the fall of Singapore.

The fearful accounts of the behaviour of the Japanese in China, which had been dinned into us for so many years, must have been a chief deciding factor with many people. It was certainly very difficult indeed for the ordinary person to know what to do. I decided that if I were told to go I would leave, but if not, I would stay. It seemed improbable that white women would be evacuated, so I went to the bank on 5 February and drew out all my own and my brother's money in the form of a bank draft, as well as a few pounds in Australian currency, the only currency the bank had left.

The streets were crowded entirely with men, both soldiers and civilians. There was hardly a woman to be seen, not even in the grocer's where I went to buy my favourite Oxford marmalade. Of course there were many Englishwomen still on duty in hospitals and aid posts, but it did appear that the burning question of whether "to stay or to go" was being treated largely as a matter for individual decision. I had not been in town for some days and the change depressed me. I decided to await orders. On the morning of Monday 9 February, I rang up Mrs. Cherry, the head of the Medical Auxiliary Service, and asked her what was expected of her European nursing staff.

"Oh," she said. "We don't know what will happen, but in the event of the worst coming to the worst we shall all be together in one of the hospitals. That is all I can tell you. We shall certainly all be together." This conversation further reassured me.

That evening a European evacuee attached as transport organiser to the staff of the Aid Post and Hospital and in charge of our pool of cars, went down to the town on business and did not come back. We waited anxiously to know if he had become a casualty in a raid, or in the shelling which had now begun in some parts of the town. Padre Adams could not find out that there had been any European casualty anywhere. Gradually we were forced to conclude that he had caught the general panic and boarded a ship, taking with him the keys of all the cars under his control, including my brother's. I had now no means of transport and did not get to the town again until the Aid Post was evacuated the following Friday. This mattered little because the shelling was then intermittent and people were asked to keep off the roads as much as possible.

On Tuesday, I was walking over from my brother's house in the school compound where workmen were rebuilding the bathroom, to Mrs. Parr's house nearby for my morning bath, when I heard a curious faint whine overhead. It was gone in a moment, and a minute later there was a gentle crash somewhere near the school buildings behind me. I could not place it at all, never having heard anything like it before. I went into Mrs. Parr's house and as I shut the front door there was another small crash, as though someone had dropped a tray full of crockery in the front garden.

We rushed upstairs together and looking out of the window saw a small hole, not much bigger than a large pudding basin, in the garden path about three yards from the house. There were more whining sounds followed by crashes farther off, and then there was silence. We had been shelled by a small mortar from somewhere in the direction of Changi, several miles away. The Japanese were not only on the island where they had been since Sunday—they were within reach. They fired off the mortar at intervals during the next few days, ten shells at a time, too small to do a great deal of damage except when there was a direct hit. There was a British battery posted in a grove of rubber trees quite close to the school, and a detachment of the Bomb Disposal Corps was quartered within the school itself, although all the former classrooms were wards full of civilian and military casualties, and a great Red Cross, made of red and white blankets, was pegged out in the compound to warn Japanese reconnaissance that the building was a hospital.

The Japanese were either trying to silence the battery or to destroy the Bomb Disposal troops. Their shelling continued at intervals and there were some hits on the buildings. One of the Bomb Disposal men was killed and another seriously injured, while one of the nursing sisters had one of those miraculous "near miss" escapes of which one hears from time to time in war. On Tuesday and Wednesday, most of the Europeans still living on the school premises or attached to the Aid Post left for the docks. They sailed off and some were killed by bombs or shells at sea. A few arrived safely in India or Australia. Some survived the sinking of the ships and were interned in Sumatra where many died. It was said that of the 42 ships which left between 11 and 15 February, the day of our surrender, only two got through.

The remaining staff at the Aid Post comprised Padre Adams, Dr. Gunstansen, Mrs. Parr and myself. All our Asian staff were still there. On Tuesday, Mrs. Parr urged me to come and stay in her house, which was a modern concrete bungalow, whereas my brother's was wooden where there was much more danger of fire. Moreover, I was alone there at night. She came over to help me pack up our things to put in her box-room. Ah Moy was still looking after me, though there was little to do as I had my meals with the European hospital staff in the school. He had been filling in his time by helping the overworked kitchen staff. He came when I was packing and, with a peculiar expression on his face, half determination, half contempt, announced that he was going home. I asked him why, rather sharply.

"*Miss mau lari,*" he answered. "*Ah Moy mau pergi rumah*" (Missy is running away. Ah Moy wants to go home).

I assured him that I was only going to stay with Mrs. Parr and told him that he might go home if he liked.

He answered, "No, if Missy is going to stay, I stay. Master would wish it. My family is all right." He was still going to and fro to them at night, though with difficulty, as the roads were barred and defended by the troops. The next day, on the advice of Padre Adams, who never forgot to look after anybody, I dismissed him to take care of his family with a month's wages, assuring him that I would be all right with the Parrs and with the Aid Post, and giving him the letter of recommendation which he had richly earned to show to any future employer. I did not see him again till after our victory.

On Thursday night, I was alone in the Parr's house as Mrs. Parr was on duty in the school, and her husband, who had come up from his military quarters, was there with her. I made my bed up in a corner at the foot of the stairs, behind some sandbags, and there lay down and tried to sleep, but it was impossible. The shelling began again, much more intense and businesslike than before. The shells flew overhead, very much louder and apparently very near. It was unbearable lying alone in the dark, so I got up and put on my uniform and my tin hat in which I took great pride and comfort. I went over to the school. The shelling had died down quite quickly and things there were very quiet. One or two soldiers came in to have scratches dressed, and as they had had nothing to eat all day I got them some bread and corned beef from the canteen. Dr. Gunstansen came and told me that orders had been received to evacuate the school the next day. The Japanese were advancing all the time and we must move into the centre of the town. He advised me to leave if I could. I did not know what to think and finally, as nothing more happened, I went and lay down on a vacant bed in one of the classrooms in which wounded and shell-shocked fugitives from Malaya were quartered, and stayed there till day came.

On Friday morning, a message came from Dr. Macgregor, the Director of Medical Services, that we were all to stay at our posts. We were all very cheerful about it.

"The Army nurses have all been sent away, and we, the civilians, are staying!" was the motif of the conversation.

About a quarter of an hour later I was in Mrs. Parr's house, packing my things for the move into the town, when one of the Hospital sisters came running in.

"We're to go!" she cried jubilantly. "Matron had just had a telephone message from the D.M.S. and we're all to go!"

"But we've just had a message that we're to stay," I said.

"Now we're to go," she unanswered. "Dr. Macgregor says that previously it was our duty to stay and now it is our duty to go." (The exact wording was possibly matron's. At any rate I was told afterwards by other women that Dr. Macgregor gave permission to go, but no orders. In any case, all was confusion at this point, as it had been all along.) "We're going at once," the sister went on. "The boat sails at 3.30."

I answered that I was not sure about going.

"Oh, well," she said. "I came over to give you the chance."

I thanked her very much for thinking about me and finished my packing. Mrs. Parr came in and confirmed the message and added that she did not think it was any use to stay any longer. She had been to the town very early that morning, and had seen the frantic panic at the docks, damage done by shelling, and our beaten soldiers standing in the streets or trying to push their way onto the ships along with local civilians. The ships were reserved for women and children only, and other soldiers, stationed there to keep order, were firing at these men to keep them off. Though previously she had been very calm, the scene at the docks had unnerved her as nothing else did. She said that everyone was going, that it was madness and useless to stay any longer. It was arranged that I should go with the Parrs in their car. As Mr. Parr was busy at the school with Padre Adams, we had to wait a little while for him.

After finishing my packing, I went up to the school to say goodbye to the people there. The nursing sisters were dragging their luggage down the stairs and out of the door, with radiant faces, while standing round the doorway and at the foot of the stairs were English soldiers in their hospital *sarongs* and *bajus*, waiting to go to town. Nobody who saw it could forget the faces of these wounded men, strangers in a strange country, as they watched the nurses leave.

I went along the passage to the Aid Post and found that our first real casualties of the war had arrived. Presumably they were shell casualties as there was no bombing near us. They lay bleeding on stretchers in the passages, and the local people, doctors and nurses, and the English doctors, were attending to them. I saw an old grey-haired Tamil, one of the schoolmasters, giving water to a wounded man, with an unforgettable expression of tenderness and sympathy on his face.

Between lack of sleep, longing to be out of it all, and the most intense shame at going, I began to cry and could not stop. I went to say goodbye to my nurses, explaining, in a vain effort to justify myself, that I was going under orders and not because I wanted to. I was comforted by the Indian doctor who put his arm round me in a paternal fashion, to the manifest surprise of the nurses who no doubt thought I was crying at the idea of parting with him. While I was waiting for the Parrs, Dr. Gunstansen came out of the treatment room for a moment, arms and apron splashed with blood, to say how glad he was that I was going to safety—all European women should go: they had done their part.

Mrs. Parr was in her car, waiting for her husband to drive us. There was no question of his leaving as he naturally had to stay with his unit. I sat in the back with the luggage and just as we were starting, Padre Adams came out with a nursing sister.

"Can you take Sister Clark with you?" he asked. "She was taking some of the wounded to the new hospital, and the others have all gone and left her behind."

She had no luggage, not even a handbag, as the luggage had gone with the rest. She had to sit on my knee as there was no other place, and the whole way down to the town she was bouncing up and down and exclaiming, "I've got to stay. I must get somewhere where I can go on with my nursing. I must get down to the Hospital!"

The roads were almost deserted except for groups of soldiers walking into the town, and in the streets through which we passed, there was little damage apparent. No one knew whether the boat was at Collyer Quay or the docks and I suggested going to the General Hospital to find out. As soon as we arrived, Sister Clark ran into the building. At the General Hospital she was in charge of a ward full of children, at the top of the building where most people would not work for fear of shells.

Standing in front of the Hospital doorway was Mrs. Bess Rogers, the Eurasian secretary of the Medical Auxiliary Service. Any orders to go applied to her as much as to me so I asked her if she was leaving.

"Oh, I'm going to stay," she answered.

"Well, if you can, I suppose I can," I said, feeling rather desperate by then, I pulled my luggage out of the car, said goodbye to my friends and went into the hospital. I never saw either Mr. or Mrs. Parr again. Mrs. Parr was severely wounded when the *Kuala* was sunk. She lost the use of one arm and was interned in Sumatra where she died. We were never told who was responsible for allowing the ships to sail during those last few days. They had no hope of reaching safety. The Japanese had complete command of the sea, and thousands of people who were lost when the ships were sunk or who died in the Sumatra camps would have lived if they had stayed in Singapore.

England Pays the Bill
June 1945

Poles and Czechs and Russians,
Europe's odds and ends,
Anti-British foreigners
Irish Free State friends,
See them share our parcels,
Share our lunch time swill,
Share our sugar, rice and oil—
England pays the bill.

Austrians and Germans,
Dutch (both white and black),
Belgians, Frenchmen, Swedes and Danes,
Gypsies from Iraq:
Disunited Nations
Clapped behind the grille,
Complicate our prison lives:
England pays the bill.

Britons in internment,
(Some have once been white),
Some are beige or coffee,
Some are black as night:
Some like walking skeletons,
Ragged, crazed and ill:
All must work at Nippon's word:
England pays the bill.

Ah, those Red Cross parcels!
From the States, from home,
Africa, Australia,
Canada, they come.
Sold by Nippon dealers,
Filling Nippon's till,
Feeding Nippon's armies,
England pays the bill.

Next, the Neutral Agent,
Buying for our good,
Smokes and talcum powder,
Odds and ends of food,
All that they allow him,
(Prices soaring still).
Someone gets a rake-off,
England pays the bill.

See the Lord of Aldgate,
Brisk and fat and spry,
From Calcutta's ghetto,
Coal-black Mordecai.
Nippon's chosen dealer,
Soaks us what he will,
Profiteers a fortune—
England pays the bill.

One-time rich Malaya
(Tin and all the rest),
Where the folk we governed
Now give Nippon best.
Ruined while our rulers
Planned with little skill.
England called our dancing-tune:
England pays the bill!

3 The White Flag

At the General Hospital I asked for Mrs. Cherry. She was my superior officer to whom I ought to report for orders if possible. She had told me that in the event of evacuating the Aid Post "we should all be together in one of the hospitals," so probably she might be at the General Hospital. However, she had sailed two or three days previously. Long after, in Changi Prison, we learned that she too drowned when her ship was sunk. I did not know anyone else to report to. The only person on the hospital staff with whom I was acquainted was Sister Uniacke. She was in charge of the Admission Ward, so I went and worked there till the hospital was evacuated.

The Singapore General Hospital was a huge place, covering acres of ground with its different buildings and roofed-in passages. The confusion there was indescribable. The Matron and many of the sisters had left earlier while most of the local-born nurses had gone home. The Assistant Matron, Miss Stewart, the remaining sisters and the rest of the nurses were carrying on as best they could with great shortage of staff. The storekeeper had left without handing over the keys and the books could not be found. The hospital was crammed with civil and military wounded and refugees. They blocked the passages, where stretchers lay loaded with the wounded, dying and dead. Some of those seeking shelter were trying to help but many merely stood about doing nothing.

Archdeacon Graham White was there organising stretcher parties along with the Bishop of Singapore and other men. Fresh casualties kept coming in. I had never seen wounds and injuries like these before and felt sick and helpless at the sight. There was plenty that the most untrained helper could do in taking round drinks of water, hot water bottles and food and making bandages and tidying up.

A dying baby of eighteen months was brought in by its father, a young Eurasian clerk. He wept and sobbed over it and told me that he had lost his wife two months previously. His sister, her children and his eldest child had all been killed by the bomb which had injured his baby. The poor baby was covered with punctures from bits of shell and died that night.

Our worst experiences followed the capture of MacRitchie Reservoir and the consequent failure of the water supply. A big Tamil coolie was brought in with a wound in the chest. All day he lay calling for water. In the evening, he suddenly haemorrhaged with a hideous rush of blood from his mouth and died. The wounded were brought in caked with dried blood and we could not even wash their faces and hands. We hardly had water to quench their parched throats.

Sister Clark's ward was occupied by some long-stay child patients transferred from the orthopaedic hospital. A large part of the ward was empty, so many stray children who were wandering about the hospital were sent to her. There was no food or water as the big glass demi-johns which ought to have been filled up for an emergency were empty and bone-dry, so she had nothing to give the children. Though Matron Stewart had told her to requisition for flour and other provisions, nothing was forthcoming.

At this point, Mrs. Graham White, wife of the Archdeacon, a former nursing sister nicknamed Nobbs, arrived at the ward and told Sister Clark that the hospital stores had been bombed and looted. She offered to send her husband to see what he could get and added, "I don't suppose he will be a very good looter because he isn't used to it."

The Archdeacon, however, proved an excellent looter and returned laden with milk and porridge. He was much pleased with his wife's praise. Slightly injured soldiers were recruited from a neighbouring ward to help feed the children. The soldiers walked along the rows of seated children and spooned gruel into their mouths from a large bowl.

There was a big British battery near the hospital. It was so close that every time it was fired, the blast of the recoil shifted our bedding on the floor of the entrance hall where we lay at night, with a queer rustling noise like ears of barley in the wind. This was in spite of a blast-proof wall across the doorway. In their attempts to silence this battery, the Japanese hit the hospital several times. We had many civilian casualties from the crowded areas round the waterfront, but the huge fires and the greater part of the structural damage were in the docks, the Naval Base, the islands that were used for oil storage, and around the airfields. Singapore town was hardly touched.

We received the news of the capitulation on Sunday night at 7 p.m. I heard of it from a Eurasian nurse as I went off duty in the black-out.

"We've surrendered!" she shouted, half hysterical with anger and apprehension. "Yes, we've hung out the white flag."

I told her to shut up (feeling rather hysterical myself) and that she was talking nonsense. Even then, many of us still believed in a last minute rescue—Wavell was coming with aircraft; the Chinese had broken through from the north; the Americans had landed at

Penang—we *knew* we could not be beaten. I was sorry that I had been so rude to the nurse and later said to her, "It's true we have surrendered, but it seemed impossible."

Work in the hospital went on but in the admission ward things were much quieter. The streams of casualties ceased, and there were many empty beds as some patients were transferred to other wards. The Japanese did not come to the hospital till Tuesday, when a senior Japanese officer spoke reassuringly to the Eurasian nurses but ostentatiously ignored the Europeans.

On Monday night, Dr. Macgregor had told us that the Europeans had three alternatives: they could stay on and continue nursing the wounded civilians for a time; they could go to the improvised military hospital in Fullerton Building and nurse the British military wounded there; or they could go straight into internment. As I was young and healthy, I felt I could not very well go straight off to internment. I had an intense homesick longing for everything English, so I volunteered to go to Fullerton Building.

Altogether six trained nursing sisters and four V.A.Ds went from the General Hospital to nurse the wounded soldiers. At Fullerton, we found two sisters and some V.A.Ds from different Aid Posts, making about eighteen women in all. Others felt that it was their duty to stay with the civilian wounded, both Eurasian and Asian. They had to move them from the General Hospital, which the Japanese wanted for their own wounded, to the Woodbridge Mental Hospital, part of which was cleared for them. This was a tremendous and heart-breaking task. The Europeans spent ten days at the Mental Hospital and were then sent into internment. There were other large groups of Europeans at Kandang Kerbau Maternity Hospital, where there were also many civilian wounded. There were groups of Europeans at the Law Courts and Raffles Hotel.

We left for Fullerton Building on Tuesday in a British Army ambulance. We had been forbidden to take any equipment from the wards as the Japanese wanted it all, but I found some ampules of morphia, syringes and needles, and some dressing forceps, which I wrapped in my handkerchief as they might be useful. As it turned out, we were not searched on this occasion and could have taken anything we liked. With transport provided, we were able to take a certain amount of baggage and a bedding roll. The unfortunate people who chose to be interned immediately had to walk from the cricket ground to a house at Katong, six miles away, with no baggage except what they could carry themselves.

I spent two and a half weeks in Fullerton Building, working in Ward 1 with Sister Uniacke. The building faced the sea but we were forbidden to look out. We occasionally peeped round the windows and saw the Chinese cleaning the streets under the direction of Japanese sentries. They covered the rubble of wrecked and bombed cars off Collyer Quay. There were between 1,700 and 2,000 wounded in the hospital. Considering everything, the organisation was wonderful. All the Queen Alexandra nurses had been evacuated by the order of Brigadier Stringer in accordance with Army Standing Orders. Many were killed when the ships were sunk or died in internment in Sumatra.

In Fullerton Building, men were dying for want of nursing. One of the V.A.Ds was an old lady of seventy, Mrs. Macindoe. She was active, cheerful and useful and very popular with the soldiers who called her "the old dear". Some of the doctors spent the whole day in the wards doing the dressings but the orderlies, particularly the night staff, were only stretcher bearers, untrained in ward work.

When we arrived, regular arrangements for cooking and for meals had been made, but for some days previously, the orderlies and other staff had been entirely dependent for their food on a volunteer canteen run by a Malay, Raja Musa, and his English wife, who had prepared whatever meals they could.

The wards, which were converted offices, were not suitable for hospital use, but we had the portable equipment of an army hospital. Sister Uniacke managed to scrounge camp beds for patients in Ward 1 after a week, but in the other wards many of the wounded were lying on stretchers on the floors. In one huge room upstairs, which had been the bar of the Singapore Club, they were so close together that one could hardly step between them. The bar and its shelves were used as a dispensary.

The Japanese did not behave with active cruelty to us. They reserved that for the Chinese. They took a large proportion of the medical stores for their own wounded, but apparently that is one of the rights of the conqueror. No food was supplied and we lived exclusively on army stores. They allowed the dangerously wounded to remain till the last minute before they were moved to the permanent P.O.W. camps at the Changi cantonments. They kept their own troops out of Singapore until all the Europeans had been sent into internment.

Great suffering was caused by the failure of the water supply, which remained very bad for a week owing to damage to the mains. Seawater was carried to the top of the six-storey building by members of the various local voluntary services connected with the army. The lavatories were gradually made usable again. It was also impossible to get a wash, and when washing patients, I had to make one very small basin of water do for three men. The men were free from prickly heat but the lack of washing facilities was very trying.

The Japanese did not interfere in the running of the hospital. I saw only three of them the whole time I was there. They were not offensive or tiresome but a sort of sick rage of anger and disgust swept over me when I saw them, so bitter was the humiliation and helplessness of defeat. This masterly inactivity was their usual policy towards us as prisoners. Having imposed certain regulations on us they did little more, but allowed us to do a certain amount for ourselves—subject to unpredictable interferences arising out of suspicion, caprice, spite and fits of ill temper.

Besides the offices occupied by our wounded, Fullerton Building contained many empty rooms full of abandoned luggage left by refugees from Malaya who had fled on board ship. During my off-duty, I used to explore these empty rooms and I quickly became a most resourceful "looter". There were suitcases full of men's clothes which helped to fit out some of the wounded who had nothing of their own to put on. One fair-haired, cheerful Cockney lad, who had lost a foot, left the building looking a perfect fashion-plate in a handsome cream silk shirt and dark red silk tie. He sat back on his stretcher, fingering the end of his tie, oblivious of the Japanese who were watching the departure, and evidently very pleased with himself and the effect he was making, as evinced by the astonished glances of other soldiers in more scruffy makeshift clothes. I had often wondered whether all that was said about the cheerfulness of the British Tommy under suffering was exaggerated, but judging from all I saw of the wounded in Fullerton Building, it was absolutely true. The soldiers in Ward 1, including about half a dozen officers, were cheerful, uncomplaining, and very independent in trying to be helpful and to do as much as they could for themselves.

There were other useful things lying about in the offices. I had brought enough bedding and clothes for myself so I filled a fair-sized trunk with sheets, pillowcases and other things which might be useful in camp, and I also found some books and various notebooks and quires of paper. The Japanese by this time had realised that there was valuable property in the offices and had written *Jangan masok*—Do not enter—

on many of the doors. I was prowling about in one such room when an unmistakable Japanese voice suddenly sounded on the other side of the partition. Snatching up a useful-looking basket, I hastily fled.

Another time, a Japanese officer suddenly came into a room where I was making a collection of men's underclothes out of a number of suitcases. He had a terrified little Eurasian man with him acting as guide, so I told the Eurasian to ask if I might have the things, thinking that perhaps he was an interpreter and spoke Japanese. Quivering with the desire to please, the little man raised imploring hands, laid his head on one side, and supplicated so abjectly that I felt highly annoyed at having asked at all. The Japanese looked confused, rather embarrassed, and finally shook his head. Had I walked off with my bundle, saying nothing, all would probably have been well, and I always regretted the loss of that haul.

One of the sisters found a small room full of St. John's ambulance equipment. We were able to fit ourselves with clean uniforms which we needed very badly. These uniforms were of strong grey cotton material. We also got straps to fasten our bundles, and useful haversacks.

Sir Shenton Thomas, the Governor, and Lady Thomas, stayed at the top floor for a short time, until the Japanese moved them elsewhere. I believe they occupied a bungalow for a few days, and then with the rest of the civilians they were sent into internment. Lady Thomas was ill with dysentery and had to go to the new General Hospital, the former Woodbridge Hospital, renamed by the Japanese as the Miyako (Victory) Hospital. The sisters and V.A.Ds whose husbands were not in Fullerton Building established themselves in some of the club bedrooms, which had private bathrooms with wash basins and showers, where we could get luxuriously clean once the water supply was put in order. For the last three nights before we left for Katong, I actually had one of these rooms to myself.

As things settled down and it gradually became apparent that for us, atrocities were not going to be the order of the day, it grew more and more trying to be shut up in the building. Hearing one day that an old Sikh was selling cigarettes up a flight of steps at the back of a store opposite, I went across the road to get some for the patients. They were English cigarettes in cartons of five hundred: Ardath, Craven A, and so on. They had probably been looted from some godown and were sold at the normal price. A little farther away, up Battery Road, Aly's, the provision merchant, was still open, but he had very little left. There were hardly any Japanese soldiers about and those present took not the slightest notice of me, so I went along Raffles Place and down Chulia Street to a shop where a Chinese grocer was selling such things as dried fruit, tinned milk, jam and biscuits.

This man was wonderful. He had a sliding ironwork gate across his shop which he kept closed, only admitting Europeans, and from him I was able to get provisions for all the men in my ward who had money to buy them. Many also wanted razors, toothbrushes and handkerchiefs, which I got from Gian Singh, whose shop was just opposite Fullerton Building, and who also obtained cocoa and other supplies which the Europeans could not go and hunt for themselves. He also sold me some tinned goods which he had kept as emergency rations "for the siege of Singapore".

An officer in Ward 1 who had only $50 asked me to get some necessary things for the soldiers who had no money, paying for them himself. When the building was evacuated, I gave him some things I had bought for my brother in the Volunteers, and asked him to hand them to my brother in the P.O.W. camp.

The shopping expeditions were amusing and exciting. The slight risk involved intensified one's satisfaction in coming back successful, having "put one over" on the Japanese. I often went out half a dozen times a day, returning with a heavy basket—my looted basket—and many loose parcels and tins. The streets were practically deserted and most of the shops were shut. There were few Japanese in our part of the city and they never molested any Europeans.

Hideous cases of cruelty and massacre occurred, but except in the case of those whom the Kempeitai Japanese secret police later took into custody on suspicion of anti-Japanese activity, European prisoners were not involved in these. I am not referring to casual beatings by drunken or vindictive sentries or to punishments for petty infringements of camp discipline, but to organised massacre, torture and brutality.

Before capitulation, Japanese soldiers bayoneted batches of English prisoners at the naval base until their own officers came along and stopped them, but on the whole, this sort of treatment was directed against the Chinese. I do not know how many hundreds or thousands were slaughtered. The Chinese themselves said thousands, the victims being mainly men in uniform, either serving with the army as volunteers or in the Auxiliary Forces as fire-fighters, lorry drivers and orderlies. Many were machine-gunned in batches with their hands tied behind them. Others were loaded into junks which were later sunk in the harbour.

In one Chinese prison camp in Sumatra, only one man escaped the general massacre. The Japanese policy was to cow and humiliate the Chinese as much as possible and to encourage the Malays, who were treated as "favourite children", but this did not last long, and later the Japanese were loathed by the Malays as well. The Malay regiment fought heroically. Malays risked their lives to help captured Englishmen, and I myself saw the joy and devotion with which Malay servants met and helped their former employers in our camp after liberation. The charges of treachery which were levelled against the Malays and other people of Malaya perhaps arose partly from the desire to find some excuse for our defeat, and partly from the ignorance among our troops of the country and its inhabitants, which led to extraordinary misunderstandings of quite simple occurrences.

We left Fullerton Building on 2 March, after all the patients had been evacuated. The very dangerously ill were left till the last, and we were able to salvage stores, which must otherwise have been left behind, by stuffing them into their kitbags or hiding them on the stretchers under blankets. Some of these surplus stores were appropriated by nurses and orderlies and provided a stand-by during the first few weeks of internment while our rations were very scanty indeed. We had to go about five miles out of the city to a seaside suburb called Katong, where the internees were packed into three large houses, overcrowded, half-starved and mosquito-ridden.

Mr. Christopher Dawson, another Englishman and I had driven out to St. Andrew's School to look for mosquito nets for the internees. Some things had been removed officially when the Aid Post and Hospital were evacuated into the town and everything else had been looted, probably before the arrival of the Japanese. The school was quite empty except for some cases of stout piled in one of the front offices, presumably placed there for their own use by the Japanese whom we could see lolling and grinning in the windows of Mr. Parr's and Mr. Adams' houses. My brother's old wooden bungalow was empty. They had not thought it worth occupying. Every stick of furniture had been looted, and not an atom of our belongings was left except a few Penguin books among a pile of torn papers on the floor. We salvaged some of these to take into internment. There was also my copy of poems by Siegfried Sasson, which I still have. As we were leaving the compound we met Lakim, the Adams' Malay syce. He stood and talked to us for a few minutes with tears pouring down his cheeks, while he enquired about Padre Adams and lamented the disaster which had befallen us all.

When we finally left Fullerton Building, the Japanese provided lorries for the nurses and also promised a military escort as a mark of respect, because we had been nursing the army, but this never turned up. We waited on the pavement outside Whiteaways' Department Store for about three hours, lunching off army biscuits, tinned pineapple, and bottles of warm beer from a small shop. A stray dog was adopted on the spot by Mrs. de Moubray, one of the party, and was with her through internment, emerging at the end quite well, but as hairless as a water buffalo owing to unsuitable food. At last Brigadier Stringer on his own responsibility ordered us to leave. We packed ourselves into two lorries full of all the luggage and equipment we had been able to get hold of, and were driven off to Katong.

Thoughts of an Old Road

The yellow grass stalks
Rustle and flutter,
Here by the road
Which is rough to my hand,
(The yellow rough road),
With a runnel of stones
In a rain-made gutter—
Beloved old road
In the far-off hills
Of my native land.

4 Introduction to Internment

Women and children who had so far been rounded up for internment, including many Eurasians, were packed into three large houses. Two had some furniture in them. The third was both empty and filthy but when I arrived, it had been cleaned up and was crowded with people. To my delight, I was greeted by a friend and her mother who I thought had left, and presently I discovered one or two other acquaintances. Room was made for me on a verandah which eight other people already occupied, closely packed and which, when it rained, was about half an inch deep in water at one end. The food was very scanty indeed. I cannot quite remember what we had to eat as I was so tired that I spent the first two days lying in the shade of a wall out of doors, trying to sleep. As far as I remember, we had a cup of tea for breakfast, a spoonful of tinned meat and a small portion of soup made from tinned vegetables at lunch, and a small cube of tinned cake and two or three pineapple chunks in the evening. The house stood close by the seashore and we were allowed to bathe every morning.

I remember very little about the three days I spent at Katong. The house was so crowded, every inch of floor space being somebody's living quarters, that I never went upstairs or even into the ground floor rooms but kept to the verandah and the bit of rough grass, enclosed by high walls, which formed the garden. We were not allowed to go to either of the other two houses occupied by the women, and of course not to whatever houses the men were in, and one could not even see them because the wall was too high. The sea was immediately beyond the wall of the garden, which must have been a great source of enjoyment to the family who had formerly owned the house. It afforded us the daily bath which was virtually our only means of keeping clean and luckily I had a bathing suit packed in my luggage.

The Japanese had been astonished to find European civilians, especially women and children, in Singapore. They did not know what to do with us. According to a speech made by a Japanese officer, Lt. Suzuki, to some of our people nearly a year later, the Army wished that "we should all disappear", but the Emperor had refused to allow this. We were therefore kept alive and later were even granted certain amenities, and in spite of poor conditions of imprisonment and a certain amount of actual maltreatment, our Camp never experienced anything comparable to Belsen and other German centres, or to some other Japanese camps in Southeast Asia.

Nevertheless, partly through what seemed to us the incapacity of the Japanese for organisation, partly through callousness and their own low standard of living, and partly through the hostility of some of those in charge of us, there was a great amount of preventable suffering and some preventable deaths. To be a prisoner is in itself a miserable condition anywhere, and for prisoners who had been accustomed to the easy life of the East and to all the privileges of a ruling race, it was an especially bitter and difficult experience. Some of the women had remained solely because they refused to be separated from their husbands, imagining that they would be allowed to live in their own houses on parole. They were separated from their husbands and did not know if they would ever see them again. Many had friends and relatives in the army and could see no prospect of ever learning whether they were alive or dead. In this respect I was fortunate as the day after capitulation, my brother had been able to walk down from the Volunteer barracks to see me in the General Hospital, where the sisters fed him with bread and cheese, so I knew that he was well.

We were very badly equipped in many ways, both individually and as a unit, but certain women were allowed to go shopping every day, doing their best to fill long orders ranging from supplies for the Camp as a whole to individual demands for bottles of red palm oil and packets of safety pins. There was no organised Committee to run the Camp nor was there a regular Commandant. The lead in dealing with the Japanese was taken by Dr. (Mrs.) Eleanor Hopkins. Later on, when we were finally settled in internment in Changi Gaol, she was the first elected Commandant of the Women's Camp. Her husband, who was also a doctor, practising in Singapore, was interned with the civilian men. At Katong, being a doctor, she was able to deal with the Japanese regarding arrangements for the sick, food supplies and sanitary arrangements.

Dr. Hopkins was a good-looking woman, small and slight, with a thin, rather long face, grey eyes and short greyish hair. She must have been in her late forties or early fifties. I do not remember ever seeing her in any clothes but dark blue trousers and shirt, except when racing round Changi Gaol at night in the wake of a Japanese officer doing a round, when she wore pyjamas and a dressing-gown. She was very "English" in voice, manner and outlook, to a point which some internees found extremely irritating. It was an Englishness of a certain kind, slightly aloof and therefore arrogant—seeming perhaps, but also courageous, clear-headed and responsible.

With the adroit support of Dr. (Mrs.) Worth, and the Men's Committee, she succeeded in getting many concessions from the Japanese military in charge of us. But for the firm stand taken by these two women and the skill which Dr. Hopkins and her male colleagues of the Men's Camp developed in dealing with the Japanese, we should undoubtedly have been much worse off in many respects than we were. Dr. Hopkins was one of the few women who brought many books into Camp. Among others, she had two anthologies of modern poetry, English and American, which she was kind enough to lend to me. This gave me great pleasure. She had had little experience of medical practice before internment, but in Changi she took on a list of patients, like the other five women doctors, in addition to her work on the Camp Committee.

In Changi, her chief friend and source of moral support was another woman doctor, Dr. Worth, nicknamed Robbie because her maiden name had been Robertson. She was a Scot, married to a Malayan planter or engineer, who was also interned in the Men's Camp. She had had plenty of experience as a practising doctor. She was a squarely-built, rather plump middle-aged woman, with a round pale face, dark brown eyes and hair, and a pleasant smile. She could be very determined (her enemies said pig-headed) but on the whole she was fair-minded in allocating the small medical "privileges" which were sometimes available, though the fact that she had control of these, and there were often not enough to go round, made her many enemies. She was always dressed in a white linen coat or overall and thus garbed, with a bag slung across one shoulder, she made her rounds among her patients. Robbie, standing with her head cocked on one side, listening attentively to people's symptoms and troubles, and replying in a quiet reassuring voice with a strong Scottish accent, was one of the most familiar sights in the Gaol.

Dr. Hopkins was succeeded as Camp Commandant by Dr. Cicely Williams, a graduate of Somerville College, Oxford, and the most brilliant and original of all the women internees. Her family were English planters in the West Indies who had been established there for generations. She liked to describe herself as a Creole, which means "one born in the country". They had suffered great reverses of fortune owning to the collapse of the West Indies economy, and it had not been easy for her to go to Oxford to get her medical training. She was about Dr. Hopkins' age, thin, of medium height, with a very fair complexion, fair hair and grey eyes, a clear, gentle voice, and a considerable sense of humour. She had worked with the Quakers investigating malaria in Greece and had done other work overseas before coming to Singapore. Her special interest was to work with children. It was she who had identified the protein deficiency disease called Kwashiorkor, widespread among children in parts of Africa where they are fed almost wholly on mealies. For this work the British Government later awarded her the C.M.G. (Commander of the Order of St. Michael and St. George).

In the autumn of 1942, Mr. Asahi, the Custodian of Enemy Aliens, asked for one man and one woman doctor to be sent out of the Camp into Singapore to write a Report on Nutrition in the city. The Camp's Medical Committee chose Dr. Williams and, from among the men, Dr. Byron to go, while Mrs. Katherine de Moubray accompanied Dr. Williams to help with the secretary work. These three were out in Singapore for several months, returning early in 1943. They lived at the Maxwell Road Customs House and worked in Mr. Asahi's office at the Chartered Bank Chambers in Raffles Place. As far as I know, no use was ever made of the Report which they drew up.

Some time after her return to Changi, Dr. Williams was elected Camp Commandant, but she held this post for a few months only. She found the tensions of our "Camp politics", the unreasonable demands and complaints, and the ill-will behind some of the problems which were raised, highly uncongenial and she resigned. She was succeeded in turn by Mrs. Nixon, by a Eurasian lady, Mrs. Chowns, and finally by an Irish nursing sister, Miss Bridget Hegerty.

I do not remember much about the short time I spent at Katong. It was in the nature of a transit camp, only used while the Japanese in the midst of their other preoccupations decided what in the world to do with us. All our living arrangements were makeshift affairs, especially the sanitary arrangements. These were very inadequate, consisting of latrines with buckets which had to be emptied into a pit in the garden twice a day, and then washed out. I was on the evening fatigue for this chore for two days and was surprised—and thankful—to find it rather less disgusting than I had expected. It was a curious fact, noticeable in many of our experiences as prisoners, that many things are far more overwhelming to read of or to see acted on stage than to experience in reality. The imagination seems to intensify what it takes hold of, while in life one is so much occupied in dealing with circumstances that their effect on the emotions is lessened. Besides, in any sort of experience, there is an interest in the novelty of things, in making the acquaintance of fresh people, and in discovering unexpected aspects of life and human nature, which is distracting and even amusing. One of my chief feelings throughout internment was surprise, very naïve no doubt, at people's inconsistent behaviour and astounding vitality. Internment was a revelation of humanity when it is stripped of pretence and of all the decorations and supports with which ordinary civilian life demands that we shall try to conceal our essential selves. I came to believe that it would be an ideal society in which one could obliterate the purely artificial and accidental values which make one person more "respected" than another.

The general condition of internment were apparent from the start, though our circumstances and organisation changed from time to time. These were: extreme overcrowding and want of privacy, inadequate food, and a general disposition on the part of the Japanese to do little or nothing for us but to permit us, though with much capriciousness and a good deal of fury and fuss, to do quite a lot for ourselves. Discomforts, privations, inconveniences, and suffering brought about by inefficiency as well as by deliberate passive hostility, were our normal lot, but there was little active ill-treatment. Nor did they, once we had arrived in Katong, ever loot our personal possessions. When we left Katong for Changi Gaol and again, more than two years later, when we left the Gaol for Sime Road Camp, all our baggage down to the smallest stick and old bottle was conscientiously transported for us, and any stealing that occurred was done by our own men and women.

When we reached Katong, our luggage was searched by Japanese officers and my tin hat was disinterred from my bedding roll where I had packed it. The officer showed some excitement over it, apparently regarding it as a dangerously militaristic object. I explained that it was a souvenir.

"Ah! Your husband!" he exclaimed, looking pityingly at me. I did not know how to explain but I wanted the hat, so I disclaimed a husband and said, "No, my brother."

"Your brother!" he repeated, still with sympathy, and gave it back to me without further question.

This was typical of their attitude to our property once we had been interned. Except for seizing some of our books after an official search in the summer of 1943—and these they returned a year later—they seemed to make a point of being scrupulously honest, as far as our personal possessions were concerned.

Our march from Katong to Changi Gaol took place on 6 March. The male internees, who had been shut up in a neighbouring house, had left the day before. Like the first internees who walked to Katong from the Cricket Ground and the second batch from Raffles Hotel, we were made to go on foot, with the deliberate intention of humiliating us before the local population, but this plan failed completely. I saw no signs of jubilation at the fall of the Europeans, only blank and downcast faces.

The walk was taken very slowly as the Japanese knew that European women were not accustomed to exerting themselves by long walks in the full tropical sun, and they did not wish to be responsible for deaths from sunstroke or exhaustion. One or two people did collapse and were given lifts on passing lorries, and transport was also provided for the sick, the aged and the very young. We carried some hand luggage such as a change of clothes, a few necessities, and rations for the day which had been issued by our own camp store. We were escorted by Japanese sentries who frequently made us stop and rest whether we wanted to or not. They were armed with rifles with fixed bayonets and appeared to carry a full field equipment of water bottles, tin hats, and other oddments slung about them. They walked in the jungle boots which seemed to be the usual footgear of their army.

Though the walk was hard on the older and more delicate women, its real sting lay in being thus publicly compelled to do something so foreign to all the ordinary standards of European activity. It was always spoken of in Camp as one of our greatest hardships and indignities, but when regarded merely as a walk it was not disagreeable. The Japanese never made me feel degraded or humiliated by anything they did to us. I had been prepared for much worse treatment, and some of them, indeed, behaved really well, while of others I thought, "Well, what can you expect of a pig but a grunt!"

The route we took to Changi lay partly along the seashore from which we could see distant islands lying blue on the horizon, with smoke rising here and there from oil dumps which had been sabotaged before capitulation. After being shut up so long indoors and in the town, with the prospect ahead of an indefinite period behind the walls and bars of a criminal's gaol, this long slow walk beside the gardens and rubber estates was something to be thankful for. Japanese troops quartered in houses along the route looked at us, grinning, but some of the officers who passed in cars turned away their heads from the marching women as though they were ashamed to look at us. The local people were going about their business as usual, pausing only to look at us with apathy or depression.

We had a picnic lunch of sardines and army biscuits under the trees at the side of the road, washed down with opaque white water which an obliging Malay drew for us from his well. Some of the Englishwomen made a point of offering biscuits to the sentries, who did not seem to have brought any rations with them. We left Katong at about 10 a.m. and did not arrive at Changi till 5 p.m. owing to the extremely slow progress insisted on by the sentries.

Although the distance was only about seven miles, we were very tired when we arrived owing to the dragging pace. I had no hat, the one I had bought at Gian Singh's having been stolen by an alert internee as soon as I arrived at Katong, and the sun brought on a headache.

As we approached the Gaol, some of the nursing sisters who were walking at the head of the procession thought they would have a joke with the sentry. Putting on a spurt they proceeded at racing speed as though they were trying to win a walking marathon. The sentry, unaccustomed to the Malayan climate and laden with equipment like the White Knight in *Alice in Wonderland*, groaned and protested, but they took no notice. In vain, he grunted and mopped his brow. They hurried on, calling to him to keep up, and puffing and panting the perspiring soldier hurried beside them.

At last the grey walls and roofs of the prison appeared on a small hill to our right. We were hot and tired and glad to see them. As we drew near, some of the women felt that a gesture of defiance was needed and they began to sing. We had left Katong singing "Tipperary" and we walked into Changi Gaol singing "There'll Always be an England", while the leaders of the procession, the better to express the unbroken state of their spirits, jumped up and down and laughed. There were Japanese officers waiting for us in the shade of the dark doorway and they gazed in amazement at these antics—the climax to the carefully planned march. They appeared wholly nonplussed.

Nocturne, May 1942

The other night I sat for hours
Upon the ledge beside the showers,
And gazed and gazed at blank infinity.
I acted in this curious way
Because I was, I grieve to say,
Just sick and tired of femininity.

I wished to be a cow, and graze,
I wished to be a pig, and laze,
I wished to be a baby elephant,
Or any other living creature
In face and habit, form and feature,
To Changi Prison most irrelevant.

By way of seeking mental change
I tried to get my mind to range

Beyond the walls, in open spaces.
I tried to contemplate the stars,
But Venus made me think of Mars—
O vanished nights! O different faces!

I never knew I loved them so,
The beery men I used to know,
The club and all its evening chatter,
The glasses chinking merrily,
While no voice rose o'er middle C,
(Excepting mine, which didn't matter).

Then I re-lived those spacious times,
The days at sea, the mountain climbs,
The shopping and the dancing.
The accidents in motor-cars,
The picnics and the talk in bars.
O days! O life entrancing!

Down! Back to earth! I gave a groan,
Then reckoned up (I checked my moan)
The blessings I could count upon.
As, yet another day was flown:
The night was fine: no female tone
Annoyed my ear, nor aircraft's drone:
A pleasant little breeze was blown.
I liked it. I had nothing on.
Yes, these were blessings, every one.
But sitting on that chilly stone
My chief delight, I freely own,
Which I'll maintain, and bate for none,
Was simply that I was—ALONE.

A view of the Gaol from the Rose Garden. Front right, the former rice-store where 100 Jewish men prisoners were quartered for a year. In the background are blocks of cells in the men's part of the prison. Painting done in internment by the author.

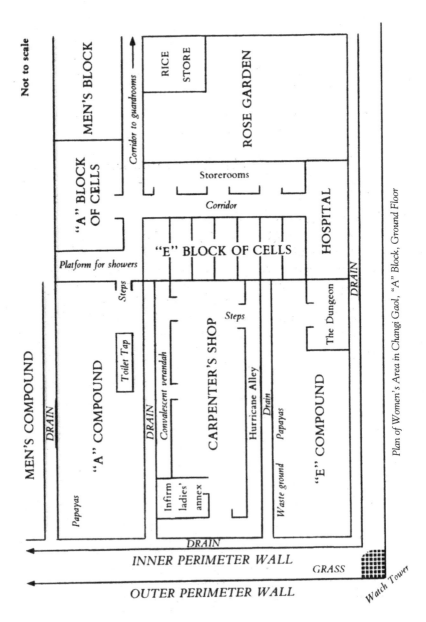

Plan of Women's Area in Changi Gaol, "A" Block, Ground Floor

5 Through the Iron Doorway

Changi Gaol was a large, modern, concrete building which had only been in use for a few years before our internment. It was surrounded by double walls, also of concrete, twenty feet high. There were a number of different blocks of cells and workshops, connected to a central yard by covered ways, the sides of which were of iron bars and expanded metal netting. Between the blocks of buildings were exercise yards. The women had the use of three yards. The prison was placed on a small hill a mile from the sea, and we always had a pleasant cool breeze in the compounds. Aesthetically, it was a very fine building even when seen from within the compounds, being beautifully designed and proportioned. Its satisfying appearance, where there was so little that was pleasant to look at, might be called one of the amenities of our lives.

There was a particularly handsome flight of concrete steps leading down to "A" Compound, which was a pleasure to look at, though wearisome and exhausting to climb up and down a dozen times a day. Inside, the building was bare, dark and damp. The cells could accommodate 600, and included a small block of special larger cells fitted with basins with running water, intended for European convicts.

It became part of the women's quarters. The prison was intended to accommodate 1,200 prisoners. The kitchen and sewerage arrangements were designed to this scale, which was fortunate for us as we totalled nearly 3,000 men and women when we arrived. This had increased to about 4,000 more than two years later.

The whole prison was lit by electricity. Every cell had a push-and-pull lavatory which, except in the European cells, was a "squatter" in Asian style. We were fortunate in having good sanitation, kitchens equipped with an adequate steam cooking apparatus, and a more or less weatherproof building. I say "more or less" because the protection from storms was quite inadequate, and in spite of projecting roofs, the rain blew into the cells through the little iron gratings. In the workshops and alleys which we were also obliged to use as permanent living space, the rain poured in practically unchecked.

"Hurricane Alley" was the appropriate name given to one such passage where about fifteen people were domiciled. All these workshops and passages were walled with concrete to a height of about three feet from the ground. Expanded metal and bars covered the space above the concrete wall.

The three storeys of cells were reached by a steep staircase of ironwork, very dark and slippery. There were twenty-two cells on each side of the passage, making forty-four per floor. At the far end of each floor was a big barred window, through which, by standing on a bench, one could get a view of coconut palms, rubber trees, and the distant sea.

The two lower floors were very dark but the top floor had the advantage of windows in the roof, admitting additional light and air. The cells had an area of 7 feet by 6.5 feet and were 11 feet high, with a central slab of concrete to sleep on, and a high grating in the outer wall and over the door. The cells were intended for one convict only but owing to our large numbers, two women shared a cell. In the case of the men, there were three of them in each cell. The larger, European cells were allotted to women with children. A number of men, including the Governor, Sir Shenton Thomas, were in a gallery of cells which our administration had considered unfit accommodation for convicts and had never been used. They were over the kitchens and ran with moisture all day from the steam from the boilers. The inhabitants, however, had the advantage of a flat roof where they could sit in the early morning and the evening, and get a good view of the countryside.

The concrete throughout the gaol had never dried properly, and the wall and sleeping slabs sweated damp. Constant airing and drying of mattresses and bedding in the sun were necessary. These had to be carried up and down the iron staircase four times a week. The building was very stuffy, particularly at night, even though we were never locked into the cells at any time and could sleep with the doors open. Many people slept out of doors in the compounds, carrying their beds in when it rained. Very few internees slept two in a cell, and those who did kept the slab as a repository for their possessions and slept on camp beds wedged into the narrow space on either side. Others slept on camp beds or mattresses on the landing outside the cells. Some of them were powerful snorers.

There were hardly any mosquitoes in the cells, but those on the lowest floor and those who slept in the compounds generally found it advisable to use mosquito nets if they had them. The concrete seemed to exude dust. This dust-laden atmosphere in the course of two years engendered certain chronic infections, such as inflammation and soreness of eyes. The prison was extremely noisy. The clatter of shoes and wooden sandals, the incessant din of human voices, the noise of people hammering, filling pails of water, clashing pots and pans, reverberated off the walls which seemed to magnify the deafening row and added to the slumlike atmosphere.

When we first arrived, we were told that the women were to occupy the European block only. Accordingly, the 400 women and children did their best to cram themselves in, the women with families in cells and the rest of us in the convicts' dining room and reading room. The allowance of space was three flagstones each, that is, about 5 by 2 feet per person, out of which we had to allow for passage space. Even so, we could not all get in. Even the Japanese saw that it was impossible, so they hastily turned out a few men who had been occupying the "A" block of cells and opened it to us.

I was among the first fifty to plunge through the iron doorway. In a surging mass, we scaled the steel staircase and tore helter-skelter along the lowest floor, each determined at all costs to plant herself in a cell before they were all appropriated by other people. I was racing in the wake of my friends down the dingy corridor, glancing into each cell as I passed and thinking that none of them looked inviting, when I noticed that one had some makeshift furniture, relics of the displaced men prisoners. I darted in and took possession. For a few days I had this cell to myself. The relief of being alone after the crowded communal life of the last few weeks, as well as of having reached somewhere permanent at last, was in comical contrast to the surroundings.

"Oh!" cried Mrs. Nelson, who came from a suffragette family, "Oh! I love my cell. I can't think why mother complained of Holloway!" Many women who were active in the campaign for "Votes for Women" before World War I were sent to Holloway Prison, and Mrs. Nelson's mother had been one of these.

Settling down to a permanent life in these strange conditions was not an easy business. We were a heterogeneous mixture of Englishwomen, Europeans married to Englishmen, Eurasians and

A cell, 11 x 8 x 7 ft. The concrete slab is for sleeping. Painting done in internment by the author.

Similar cell as fitted up by two women. Painting done in internment by the author.

Asians married to or connected with Englishmen. Many of us were total strangers to one another, while others were already acquainted in varying degrees. This meant that the feuds as well as the friendships of normal life were imported into the gaol. The chief of these feuds was the old-established jealousy of the business community for members of the Malayan Civil Service. Also, some of the wives of heads of departments were determined not to give up the prestige which, in normal life, they struggled so hard to maintain over women whose husbands were less rich or less senior in their jobs. The pressure of circumstances eventually reduced this determination, but not for some time.

There was also jealousy of the doctors' position. The easiest, often the only way, to obtain necessities and concessions from the Japanese was to put them forward on grounds of health. The Japanese had a certain respect of the medical profession. If the doctors were insistent enough in their demands, they could obtain a good deal for us. This gave them an importance greatly envied by some others. Under these circumstances, there were other difficulties in the way of smooth organisation. The Japanese washed their hands of all details in the running of the camp and told us to manage everything ourselves.

The first thing we had to do was to elect a committee, arrange hospital accommodation for the sick and make the most of the cell and corridor accommodation and apportion it out fairly. As soon as we reached the gaol, we were summoned to a meeting in the convicts' dining-room by Dr. Hopkins. Standing on a concrete table, she told us that the Japanese had ordered us to do our own cooking. She asked for volunteers for this thankless job. Eight people offered to help. It was hard work as there were no cooking facilities in the women's part of the gaol. We had to cook on six open fires built up on bricks, partly sheltered from storms under the verandah of the Carpenter's Shop. We washed our rice in four changes of water at the edge of the concrete drain which ran under the verandah platform. For utensils we had some large iron army cooking pots, two frying pans, and a wooden spoon with which the rice was stirred when necessary. We had two kerosene tins in which soup was boiled. Our menu was as follows:

Breakfast: A mug of tea with sweetened condensed milk, made in the men's kitchens and sent to us in the prison water-cart.

Lunch: A small cupful of cooked rice and two tablespoonfuls of thin watery soup made out of assorted tins from our own camp stores.

Dinner: A small cupful of *kanji*, that is, rice pap, made with condensed milk, and perhaps four pineapple cubes each or a couple of biscuits.

The internees could not grasp the fact that there really was no more food than this available, and leapt to the conclusion that the kitchen staff were secretly battening on all sorts of illicit extras which should have been added to the general meals. There was no truth in this notion, but it was the first indication of one of the most typical features of our life as internees—accusing everybody in any responsible position of all sorts of malpractices and abuse of "privileges", merely as an outlet for the discontent, disappointment and unhappiness with which the camp was seething. Later on, people became accustomed to this atmosphere of violent criticism and knew what to expect, but at first it was rather a shock, especially as the most energetic attacks generally came from those who were themselves doing least to help.

The scanty menu and troublesome cooking arrangement continued for three weeks, after which the Japanese gave permission for the men to cook for us in the electrically equipped prison kitchens, where there were steam boilers and other facilities. At the same time, our store was amalgamated with theirs and the daily rations for the two camps were planned on the same menu. They were soon able to increase our rations, and when the Japanese gave permission for some men to go to Singapore town on shopping expeditions, our food became comparatively adequate, though not very palatable to European tastes. We had bread, sometimes brought in from town, sometimes made by the men from rice flour which was ground in the gaol, or from other cereals such as maize and, later on, from millet, ragi and soya bean.

In spite of the efforts of the men cooks to provide us with "bread" of some sort, from time to time, throughout internment, I had a special craving for the bread we baked at my village home in Gloucestershire. It was crusty wholemeal bread, made from wheat grown on local farms and stone-ground by a mill on the little River Evenlode, in the valley below us. The flour was bought a sackful at a time and emptied into a large bin which stood in a corner of our 600-year-old rectory kitchen. Sometimes when my mother was baking, we were allowed to make our own "little loaves", consisting of a round handful of dough, well-kneaded, with a smaller round pressed down on top, the top one being slashed across with two cuts from a sharp knife to give it a proper baker's look.

The loaves were first of all put to rise above the wide black kitchen range which stood in a recess in the wall, well out of draughts, and then baked in the oven till they were cooked, with a beautiful crust on their outside. We ate them with golden-yellow butter, made by the farmer's wife in the village and left at the house twice a week by a child on the way to school. Sitting in my cell, eating the daily rice-porridge or rice-bun, I remembered those loaves and that butter more lovingly than any other pre-internment food.

A great deal of our food in those days was local-grown. Milk came from another farm next door, and I was sometimes sent with a milk can to fetch it. Occasionally I arrived too early and would watch the farmer at his milking. First, he washed his hands in cold water at the pump in the yard. Then he sat on a low stool to milk the cows. Occasionally a bit of dried mud fell off the side of the cow into the milk pail. He carefully picked it out and then carried on. These were shocking conditions by modern standards of hygiene, but we never suffered any harm from the milk. Beef and mutton (no one ate lamb in those days) were locally grown, and of course the butcher made his own pork sausages with which no modern, factory-made sausage can compare.

Most people kept their own pigs and chickens and everyone grew their own vegetables and some fruit. We had a gardener-handyman whose work included two hours pumping night and morning to bring water from our own well into the house. The pump stood in a small stone pumphouse where one could hear the water pouring into a large concrete tank, from which it was piped to hot and cold water tanks in the house a few yards away. On Sundays, when the gardener had the day off, the household had to take turns at the pumping, we children being strictly told to imitate his slow, even, rhythmical strokes and not to try to hurry, because the water must have time to flow. Thus, even our water supply was locally produced, and it too was very good. These far-off days, the background to my life, were often present in my mind in the equally "primitive" though very different circumstances of life in Changi Gaol.

With care, our stocks of tinned beef and sardines at Changi lasted for nearly two years. They were almost our only protein source except for eggs, which were sometimes obtained through a dealer. These were generally Chinese preserved eggs and were often far from fresh. Fruit was rare and there was a shortage of fats. Stocks of tinned butter and margarine were eked out with the utmost economy. When they were finished, we had to rely entirely on the regular supplies of red palm oil, which we ate with our rice, or mixed with our soup, or took neat by the spoonful. Throughout internment, rice was our staple cereal, and a lunch of steamed rice and sweet potato-leaf soup was the chief meal of the day.

The men brought the food to the Carpenter's Shop where we waited in four long queues of about seventy people each. A sentry was always on duty to see that no illicit conversation took place between the men and women. In spite of this, extra food in the shape of special bread, tins of fish and meat and fresh eggs, all stolen from the camp stores, were often delivered by the food fatigue to the wives of men who worked in the kitchens. The sentries were often thoroughly bored with their supervision and the enforcement of petty restrictions. Later on, when we were allowed to have a piano, the sentry would generally sit down at it while we were queuing and pick out tunes with one finger. The favourite with all sentries was *Auld Lang Syne*. As sure as the strains of *Auld Lang Syne* were audible from the Carpenter's Shop, we knew that some fatigue accompanied by a sentry was about, and we prepared to mind our p's and q's accordingly.

The gaol was quite bare except for some heavy work-tables and carpenters' benches. Some people were able to equip themselves with the prison wardens' furniture which was stored in a lumber-room, but the majority had nothing but the bare concrete to sit or sleep on for some time. The lumber-room itself was taken over by some nursing sisters as their quarters. It had a very low roof and little ventilation and was named the Dungeon. A small boy in the course of his lessons was asked to explain what a dungeon was, and he answered, "A place where nurses sleep!" Another small lumber-room dormitory, being very dank and dark, was known as the Crypt. The dining room was much too small for our numbers, and later became the children's school-room. Some of us ate our meals in the cells, some in corners of the compounds or the Carpenter's Shop, propping ourselves against ledges or sitting at the edge of the drains. These drains were unlike those in England. They were intended to carry off the water which poured from the roofs during a storm and if swept daily, were fairly clean.

As things settled down, the men were permitted to go out on fatigues to collect wood for the kitchens, equipment from abandoned houses, and other junk and lumber from which they made stools, small tables and other necessities. In the end, we were quite well furnished in a makeshift way, but it took about a year. The older people and those with friends who had a pull, had folding chairs with backs of canvas or sacking, little tables for bridge or meals, and small cupboards made of old packing cases. Shelves were fitted in the cells, and camp beds were bought in the town or made in the gaol by the carpenters. One day a drunken Japanese burst into a particularly well-furnished cell and found the men playing bridge. The sight of so much comfort among the "criminals" (as they told us we were) outraged his feelings deeply, and he proceeded to lay the place to waste and knock the men about. When he had gone, they put up a sign: PEARL HARBOUR.

People's health suffered from the first, some disturbance being due to the misery of defeat and imprisonment as well as to the physical hardship and unaccustomed food. There was an outbreak of dysentery. The patients were sent to the Miyako Hospital which was in the charge of local-born doctors and nurses, with one or two English doctors permitted to remain and work there. With some internees, their hatred of the prison life expressed itself in a nervous, panic stricken fear for their health.

Symptoms of beri-beri were detected by women who had never come across a case of it in their lives, while such words as malnutrition, calories, vitamins and pellagra were bandied about on all sides. Finally, Dr. Cicely Williams was constrained to give a series of soothing health talks. She tried to quiet the extremes of the constipation panic by telling us about a famous old Arab who suffered from this condition for over a year without a break, and was apparently hale and hearty at the end.

Constipation remained a troublesome problem with many people throughout internment, the diet being very deficient in fresh fruits. A system of monthly weighing was instituted, with a view to giving some people some extra diet if they showed alarming losses. This unfortunately increased the panic, as some women, even if they started considerably overweight, considered every pound loss as one step nearer to the grave. However, once the diet had settled down on a moderately reasonable scale, and once people had grown acclimatised to the unusual conditions of life, some internees actually seemed to benefit by the enforced austerity.

The food for this earlier period might be considered a good-class Asian diet, even if it was not what Europeans were accustomed to in quality and quantity. It was sufficient for health in the tropics. It remained at this standard until October 1943. During the last few months of this period, it was supplemented by a weekly sale of fresh fruits and vegetables. The internees could cook the vegetables according to taste on special wood-burning stoves as they pleased. An extensive market in cooked food, such as curries, vegetable pies and so-called doughnuts, grew up among the Asians who were experts at this sort of cookery and made a big profit on their wares.

After the Kempeitai took over the camp in October 1943, the food became increasingly deficient both in quantity and quality. At no time did we have fresh milk for the children or enough invalid food for the sick. The camp was given tinned milk in its tea for the first few months, after which the men's store decided that it must be kept for the children and the sick. Soon after we moved to Sime Road in May 1944, milk had to be restricted in very small quantities to the youngest children.

The doctors' special position was not always plain to the laity, some of whom disagreed loudly with the doctors' directions, and complained with great indignation because details of the patients' condition were not published for general discussion. In some cases, the prejudice and criticism amounted to petty persecution. It is not an exaggeration to say that there were women in our camp who owed the preservation of a degree of health and, in the long run, perhaps even their sanity and their lives, to the firm stand made by the doctors on their behalf. The resentment of some internees at any alleviation of the lot of others, on whatever grounds, was incredibly bitter, especially of attempts to make life more tolerable for the sick, the old and infirm, and the children.

The women's hospital was housed in a stuffy room which had formerly been the European prisoners' library. The corridor was fitted with a peculiar system of water supply. Whenever anyone drew a cup of water in any cell, a tremendous rumble reverberated along the whole passage, while the screams and shouts of the children who lived in these cells also added to the amenities of life in hospital. By persistent badgering of the Japanese, Mrs. H. I. Worth succeeded in getting the hospital equipped. With the co-operation of the men's committee, she and Dr. Hopkins, our first women's Commandant, managed to browbeat and bamboozle the Japanese into providing, or letting us scrounge, two electric stoves, a refrigerator, a long bath with a geyser, wheelchairs, beds, mattresses and other equipment.

A section of the "A" compound verandah was taken over for convalescent patients and converted into a very useful outdoor ward, with bamboo blinds which could be lowered to keep out the rain. A small room on the ground floor, known as the Infirm Ladies' Annexe, was taken over as a ward for old and crippled women who were looked after by V.A.Ds. and by some of the Little Sisters of the

Poor who were interned later. In addition, Dr. Worth got permission for a small bungalow to be transported piecemeal by our men into "A" compound, and there rebuilt by them as a sanatorium for chronic and tuberculosis cases, whose numbers increased as time went on. All these developments came in for indignant criticism from one or another section of the camp. The building of the sanatorium even brought a threat of an appeal to the Japanese from women who were accustomed to playing bridge in that particular spot every evening. However, they resigned themselves to playing bridge in one of the other compounds instead, and thought better of the appeal!

Special arrangements had to be made by the various camp authorities regarding the ambulance which went out regularly from the camp to Miyako Hospital, and to Kandang Kerbau Hospital. A trip on the ambulance was a much envied pleasure, partly as a change from the gaol, partly because we could do a little shopping if the sentry was well-disposed. From the Japanese point of view, all such shopping was strictly forbidden and was liable to punishment. It says much for their confusion of mind regarding the treatment we were to have that, in spite of an occasional outburst, they winked at this illicit shopping for many months. In practice, there were very few in the women's camp who did not at some time or other benefit from the extras obtained in this way.

The strain and risk of the ambulance shopping were very great. Some who went out would not undertake it at all, as it was quite impossible to make it an equal facility for everyone, and any system of distribution entailed severe criticism, while there was always the possibility that the Japanese might suddenly decide to punish all concerned. Second Lieutenant Takuda, second-in-command of the camp, a roaring bull of a man, one day complained bitterly to Dr. Hopkin about the conduct of women who had been allowed to go to Miyako, ostensibly to consult specialists there. Apparently he considered himself a specialist in manners.

"The ladies," he lamented, "do not behave like ladies. When they come back, instead of coming to thank me for letting them go, they hurry away with large bags of shopping which they had no business to buy!"

The disputes about the ambulance increased, and on the whole it was a relief when the Japanese put a stop to the illegal shopping altogether.

The care of the children was another thorny topic and remained so for the whole of our time in Changi. Dr. Bowyer of the men's camp, who was in charge of the diets, insisted that the camp as a whole was responsible for the children's health and welfare. Under his direction, they were given whatever extra rations were available, on a scale graded according to age. These included eggs, tinned milk, fruit, extra "bread", special soup and other odds and ends, the kind and quantity of the extras varying from time to time according to what was obtainable. This policy was subjected to continual and violent criticism from some women on the grounds that a few of the mothers sold the children's extras to other internees in order to get money to buy cigarettes, or for gambling. This abuse became so bad that in 1943, a number of women volunteered to supervise the children's meals in the prison dining-room, so as to make sure they got the food intended for them. But the suggestion came to nothing, partly because the organisation of feeding arrangements on these lines was rather difficult, partly because the camp authorities feared to antagonise the children's mothers and so lose their votes in the camp elections. Still, on the whole, thanks to the extras, and to the care taken by Dr. Margaret Smallwood and Sister Farrer who were in charge of their health, the children were vigorous and well developed and did the camp great credit.

At various times, women came in pregnant, and altogether about twenty babies were born in the camp. The restriction of prison life was hard on the children in spite of all efforts to mitigate things for them. As soon as it could be arranged, school was organised by various professional teachers, first by Mrs. Milne, and when she was too ill to continue, by Miss Renton. Some of the children made very good progress in spite of a shortage of textbooks which severely handicapped the teachers.

Mrs. Stanley-Cary ran a Froebel class for the tiny ones for almost the whole period of internment, and as soon as space could be found, a crêche for the babies was opened by Mrs. Loveridge and Sister Muriel Clark. A grass-covered compound, known as the Rose Garden because we thought it had a rather refined air though no roses, was given up as a children's playground, and here they yelled, danced about and played games. There was a room with a flat roof abutting on this compound where the Japanese would sometimes sit in the evening, watching us and occasionally throwing sweets to the children. We hated to see the ensuing eager scramble and hear them whining for more, especially as some of the sweets seemed to have come out of stolen Red Cross parcels.

It was interesting to hear the various reasons which had led different women to stay and face the chances of capture by the Japanese. Some had stayed for purely personal and romantic reasons—to be with a husband or fiancé. Others like the doctors and nurses, the school teachers and missionaries, had remained to do a definite job of work which they felt they could not leave, while a few had remained out of love and loyalty to the country itself. Mrs. O. R. S. Bateman, an elderly and delicate woman, once said to me, "My husband and I have been twenty-five years in Malaya. The country has been very good to us. I wasn't going to run off and leave it as soon as it got into difficulties."

It needed a high degree of self-restraint and public spirit if internment under our crowded and enclosed conditions was not to be a hell on earth. It sometimes was hell when ill-feeling was industriously fomented and minor mistakes magnified out of all recognition by people who wanted to catch the votes of the discontented at the next camp elections. Feeling at these times ran furiously high.

People quarrelled with their friends or avoided them for fear of quarrels and some got into such a state of nervous excitement that they could not sleep at night. Terrible "camp scandals", grounded in the most trivial reasons or no reason at all, were earnestly and bitterly discussed, and feuds and hatred manifested themselves in all sorts of unpleasant, petty ways which under our conditions, sometimes amounted to real cruelty.

Yet as each crisis subsided, to be followed in a few days, weeks or months by a fresh one, we could laugh at ourselves for a little while and say, "Of course, once we're free we shall forget all this, or if we do remember, it will be to wonder what on earth all the fuss was about." At the time these quarrels were recognised as having a good side since they were at least a symptom of vitality. Later on, when semi-starvation began to take effect, as well as prolonged monotony and boredom, people grew too tired and apathetic either to give or take offence.

For me there was from the first, a special mitigating circumstance in having to live in a gaol, because for many years I had been interested in prisons and the life led by prisoners. I have no idea how I came to have this interest, but in my first year at Oxford University, when I was about nineteen years old, I read two books on prisons which had nothing to do with my degree course in Modern History but which I found absorbing. One was a study of the prison system by Sydney and Beatrice Webb, the noted socialists, and the other, more human in its approach, was published by the Howard League, the Quaker group concerned with prison reform. I remember little of these two books now, except that in the Quaker study of prison and its effects on prisoners there was a description of a negro who for some reason was incarcerated in a police cell for a time, and who after a while appeared to go out of his mind. He remained quiet, gave no trouble at all, but became absorbed in making patterns on his black skin with the porridge, and he took no notice of anything else. There was no suggestion of ill-treatment by the police. This was simply the result of solitary confinement for a prolonged period—something which affects different people in different ways. "Is this really part of prison?" I had thought. "Ought we to allow this to happen—do this to people?"

Because of this long-standing interest, I did not find it entirely time wasting to spend a period as prisoner in a gaol myself, though under very different circumstances from those experienced by the ordinary prisoner. These were in some ways better and in some ways worse. For one thing we had excellent sanitation, something very different from the insanitary conditions obtaining in most English gaols. We were much more overcrowded than in any English prison but since we were never locked into our cells, we had more personal freedom and normal activity, and no one suffered the strain of solitary confinement. The long-term effects of prison, however, are the same for all prisoners. These are: being shut in, absence of any foreseeable future, and the loss of one's liberty.

Camp life was also full of touching and surprising kindness. Perhaps, in a way, none of us will ever have happier birthdays than those we spent in internment. Anniversaries called out everything that was most friendly and sympathetic in people's natures. All sorts of people offered their congratulations. Little presents and small celebrations were always contrived, at far more cost to the giver than the most expensive fetes and treats of ordinary life. A most festive and hilarious party spirit reigned on these occasions, though the refreshments mostly consisted of food saved from the daily rations and made more attractive by private re-cooking, supplemented perhaps by the contents of a long-cherished tin, or a few eggs or some fruit secured on the quiet by judicious wangling. Later on, when there was no milk for the coffee, not even coconut milk, and the refreshments consisted of biscuits made of the pounded lunch rice flavoured with curry powder, or of some raw salad grown in a private patch of garden, our zest for these parties was, if anything, greater than before.

It was this atmosphere of generous kindness and friendly warmth, the happiness of finding that even through the universal sense of misery which underlay all our activities, people could always find it in themselves to give up something and contrive something to give pleasure to a friend, which made our birthdays some of the most unforgettable experiences of internment.

Internment, Six Months

All the long day the wind blows cool,
Blows from the imprisoned sea,
That sleeps and surges, wanders free,
Swings with the tide, and knows no rule
Beyond its timeless liberty:
Here we are bound in a hard school.

For here are partings, and here the pain
Of hope deferred, and each long, long day
Dies unheeded: we go our way
As through a dream, uneasy, vain,
And always the grim, monotonous grey
Of the high walls shuts us in again.

We see the sky where the clouds sail,
Drifting down in the changing light,
And vagrant birds pass through in flight,
And rain sweeps up with the racing gale,
And memory-stirring, star-strewn night
Comes with her quiet, her dark-blue veil.

We wait for a day: the day we go
Out through the gates where life still calls:
Out where the windows are bare, and the walls
Are homely again: where the winds blow
Through familiar trees, and the sunlight falls
On flowers and faces of long ago.

Barbed wire outside the gaol. Line drawing done in internment by the author.

6 Dealing with the Japanese

We gradually settled down into some sort of routine and order, though in a sense, our life was never settled since no one ever knew what the Japanese were going to do next. From the beginning they told us we were to organise our camp ourselves, but the officer in charge of us had a right of veto and general interference. Two rules were laid down: (1) everyone had to work, and (2) no racial distinctions were to be made.

Under the circumstances, these were not unreasonable. They also strictly forbade any communication with the men, but on the whole, this rule was successfully evaded. Husbands, relatives or friends in the men's side of the gaol were continually coming into our camp to do jobs as plumbers, carpenters and electricians. Thus, there were frequent opportunities for communication. Every now and again, after an illicit note had been intercepted or a sentry had slapped a woman's face for too obviously talking to her husband, the Japanese would take some action, beating a man, or furiously haranguing the men's and women's representatives, or stopping all fatigues from coming into the women's camp for a day or two.

The first Women's Commandant, Dr. M. E. Hopkins, believed in being firm with the Japanese, and firmness when combined with tact and adroitness produced on occasions surprisingly satisfactory results. Our captors were puzzled and embarrassed as to how to treat us. They had not been allowed to kill us off. They did not quite know where to draw the line in their general treatment.

Partly through ignorance and inefficiency, partly because they disliked us and did not want to do more for us than they had to, they hardly suggested any practical arrangements themselves. Everything had to be obtained through repeated requests made by the authorities of the two camps. They complained bitterly that we were always asking for things. They told us that we ought to be "more spiritual" (like themselves, they added), and not to want so much. They called the official interview which our Commandant had with them daily, "Askings".

With the heads of the men's and women's camps backing each other up, and reinforced by the medical staff, a formidable combination was presented to the Japanese who were continually being told that Europeans could not stand this and must have that. As they did not know what dire results might follow a refusal, they frequently ended by giving way. After a time we were, within the limits of our unsuitable quarters, not too badly off. Food, mostly purchased out of camp funds, was reasonably adequate. Gradually we were equipped with such indispensables as bedding, a stool, eating utensils, and some sort of receptacle for washing clothes and storing water. The latter was essential as the water supply was not constant and went on and off in a rather haphazard fashion.

The Japanese at first tended to wander in and out of the camp at all hours. Dr. Hopkins represented strongly what a heinous and unheard of thing it was that men should roam about a women's camp at night. She assured them that they would get a shocking bad name among civilised nations if they continued to permit it in a camp of

Englishwomen. Finally, they agreed that the door connecting the women's quarters with the central yard and the rest of the gaol should be locked every evening, and that she should keep the key. This arrangement lasted for some time and the Japanese hardly ever came round our quarters at night although they retained a second key.

Whenever a Japanese wandered round our camp after dark, which they did out of curiosity or an oafish desire to be tiresome when we were bathing under the open-air showers and going to bed, the Camp Commandant and her Deputy were always called by the person who saw them. They accompanied the intruder wherever he went until he took himself off again.

Some of the Japanese accepted this escort quite as a matter of course and would wait at the gate for Mrs. Hopkins to make her appearance before they set forth. Others grumbled about it but they never dared actually to forbid it, being quite aware that they had no business in our quarters at those hours. Women who slept on the concrete outside the cells were naturally alarmed when a prowling Japanese stumbled over them in the dark, especially as these were often drunk. It was reassuring to find him accompanied by a camp official instead of being left entirely to his own devices.

The practice was continued by Dr. Williams who succeeded Dr. Hopkins, but later Commandants dropped it as it was a great deal of trouble. It did, in fact, require a good deal of courage as some of the more unpleasant Japanese were very angry at being thus supervised. Probably it had a restraining influence on the Japanese in their general attitude to us. At any rate, it was only after it had been dropped for some time, and they had formed the habit of coming in and out quite freely, that they began to form the liaisons with some of the young Eurasian women which, blossoming undisguised at Sime Road, added very greatly to the trials of our lives.

While the Japanese were thus receiving what might be called a training in English rules of conduct, in other directions they imposed their own ideas on us. We were strictly told to cease using the expressions "Japan" and "Japanese", and must say "Nippon" and "Nipponese" instead. Among ourselves, we shortened the latter word to "Nips". They were very particular about the use of these terms, Japan and Japanese being Western expressions and as such highly objectionable to them. After three years of internment, a stoker from the *Empress of Asia* received a postcard from a friend who wrote: "I hope those bloody bastards of Japanese are treating you properly." The Japanese censor read this and the man was summoned to the office. He went, expecting to be beaten up for his friend's bad language. Instead he was told that he must inform his correspondents that they were not to speak of "Japanese"—"Nipponese" was the correct term. The rest passed quite unnoticed.

Another beneficial innovation was the order to advance all clocks two hours in accordance with what was called "Tokyo Time". This gave us an extra two hours of daylight in the evening though it often meant getting up in the dark. To have twilight till half past eight every night instead of only till half past six was a real advantage. In Singapore, the times of daybreak and sunset vary within about half an hour. At one time of year it would be quite light when we got up at 7.30 a.m. (Tokyo Time), while later on it was not light till nearly 8 a.m.

A very important rule was that we must bow whenever we met a Japanese—and bow properly, inclining the body from the hips with heels together and hands straight along the sides. The Japanese had no sense of humour on the subject of bowing. It was their national salutation, a fundamental rule of polite manners, and they naturally took it very seriously. At roll-call, we were supposed to bow in unison, bareheaded and silent, on the arrival of the officer in charge. The men

Internees were forced to bow to the Japanese guards. Scene re-enacted after liberation.

became quite expert at this but the women never succeeded in giving satisfaction. To the end, their bow was lamentably ragged, while the sacred silence was punctuated by illicit whispers and shuffling, in spite of threats, cajolery and impassioned appeals to our *esprit de corps* by the Japanese in charge of the ceremony who longed to feel proud of us.

Some of the women never became reconciled to bowing. They considered it a great humiliation and whenever possible made a special point of either not doing it at all or of doing it as badly as possible. The Japanese themselves were far from punctilious in acknowledging our bows. They usually saluted a Eurasian or an Asian but they often walked past the Europeans with their noses in the air, however elegant a bow they had received. The unfortunate camp officials were always being hauled over the coals because of our unsatisfactory bows, and occasionally a woman who had failed to bow quickly enough got her face slapped.

Our first Japanese Commandant was Lt. Okasaki, a Presbyterian who had smooth manners and seemed more friendly than he really was. His aide was 2nd Lt. Takuda, a noisy, hot-tempered person, who was nevertheless more popular than Okasaki because we knew where we were with him. His bark was worse than his bite. He used to go careering through the camp with long rapid strides, shouting indignant complaints, while our Committee ran gasping in his wake trying to catch up and make out what he was saying.

After these two, we had for a few months a remarkably humane and sympathetic man called Mr. Naito, while at the same time a man of similar kindly and civilised disposition, Lt. Suzuki, was in charge of all the enemy aliens in Malaya. During their regime, various concessions were made to us or were initiated, and the whole atmosphere of the camp was different from anything either before or after.

When Lt. Suzuki was moved after a few months to another post, he came to Changi for a farewell visit. He met Dr. Williams who had been Commandant during his regime and shook hands with her with tears in his eyes, warning her that some very harsh people "who would be anxious to punish you" were coming to take charge shortly, and saying that he hoped she would be all right. He was succeeded by the Kempeitai. Mr. Naito paid with his life for his kindness. After the Double Tenth, when the Kempeitai took over and all our privileges were withdrawn, Naito was shot for being "too kind" to us.

Natio's successor was Mr. Tominaga, who remained in charge of us till the end. He definitely disliked Europeans, because, so camp rumour went, he had been ill-treated by Americans when he was wounded while fighting in Shanghai. He was a more rough and brutal type than any of his predecessors and in fact was connected with the Kempeitai, but for the first few months he interfered very little with the routine of the camp and permitted most of the privileges, which Mr. Naito had granted, to continue. He claimed to have been educated at Berkeley University in the United States, and was a great reader of Somerset Maugham and other well-known English writers, and spoke very good English. He was a bully when drunk or irritated and used to knock the men about sometimes in his tours of the Camp. After we moved to Sime Road, very little was seen of him. He left the running of affairs almost entirely to his subordinates. After he became Commandant, he refused to speak English to our officials, and all Camp business had to be conducted in Malay, or in Japanese through a European interpreter.

Tominaga was a curious person. He had a bad reputation among the men for roughness and violence but at times he belied it in the most unexpected way. A man internee who had somehow illegally retained possession of a pair of binoculars, one day climbed onto the roof of the main block cells, and spent a quiet half hour there with the binoculars gazing over the countryside. He was seen and taken before Tominaga who deprived him of the binoculars and dismissed him. For about twenty-four hours, the Camp was in a ferment expecting to hear that he would be beaten to death, but nothing further happened till one day he arrived to see me at the Relatives' Meeting. He said, "I had to pass Tominaga in the yard and he makes me very cross. Ever since they caught me on the roof, whenever he sees me he points at me and dances up and down and laughs, and I don't like it!"

I was once summoned before Tominaga on account of some lines of verse which had been published in the Women's Camp magazine, *Pow-Wow*. I had to read these aloud to him, which I did with the Men's and Women's Commandants standing on each side of me with a dreamy, distant expression on their faces. I read with a dead-pan face, in a flat, monotonous voice as instructed beforehand by Cicely Williams who was Women's Commandant at the time. The poem was called *Changi Lullaby*. The "clashing chains" mentioned were not fetters, but the lavatory chains, which were constantly being pulled throughout the night owning to the diuretic effect of our rice diet.

> Little Internee, sleep sound in thy bed,
> The concrete, like granite, supports thy thick head:
> The clash of a chain or the blast of a snore
> Will sweeten thy rest in the dust of the floor.
> The fatherly face of a foe on the prowl
> Will haply illumine thy cell with a scowl,
> While out in the compound the rain and the dew,
> The cats and mosquitoes are company too.
> Hushabye, darling, (while cockroaches creep) . . .
> Little Internee, why aren't you asleep?

Tominaga had taken exception to this because it might give an erroneous idea of conditions in the Camp. He told me to confine my jokes in future to subjects unconnected with internment. Apparently he had imagined that it had been written by Lady Thomas, though we were not related in any way. I had to give various particulars to prove that Thomas was my real name and that I was not a stooge for someone else. After this interview, whenever we were lined up in alphabetical order for roll-call and Lady Thomas and I therefore stood side by side, he always ginned and nudged his *aide-de-camp* in the ribs, his eyes twinkling at some private joke mysteriously connected with the two of us. We could never make out what amused him so and came to the conclusion that the Japanese sense of humour was incomprehensible.

The Japanese were very insistent that Lady Thomas must be treated on the same level as the other internees, but general feeling in camp caused the privilege of a private cell to be given to her, of which apparently the Japanese did not know—at least they never interfered. They were always on the look-out for any action on her part to which they could take exception, but as she lived in the same way as the rest of us, and took no part in the management of the camp, they were unable to find fault.

Punishments by the Japanese were various. Sometimes the men were beaten, as in the case of one who was caught after climbing the wall several times to visit a lady friend in a neighbouring *kampong* (village). Dr. Johns was locked in a lavatory for two days for some imaginary offence, and Dr. Williams was put in the Guard Room for some hours on similar grounds. A favourite punishment was to shut people up for a day without food. Women who were caught talking to men or smoking in the corridors, or who failed to bow properly to a passing sentry were liable to have their faces slapped. Privileges might be withdrawn from the whole camp, or the men were prevented from coming over on necessary fatigues.

On the whole, the crimes that were punished and those left unpunished were equally unaccountable. The behaviour of the Japanese in authority seemed to be dictated chiefly by the mood of the moment or their personal feelings towards the individual involved. Official beating-up of internees was quite rare. In Sime Road on different occasions, various sentries took a particular spite against one man or another because the affections of one of the girls was involved and they took it out on their rivals. I saw one of these "beatings-up" which took place outside the women's hospital at Sime Road, the ostensible reason being unnecessary conversation between the man, who was a member of the food fatigue, and the hospital Matron. The sentry punched the man lightly on the shoulder a number of times, but in fact scarcely touching him. Obviously he was trying to provoke a return punch which would have entitled him really to set on his rival, but the internee remained stiffly at attention, his chin in the air and his hands at his sides. The sentry had to go away disappointed. At Sime Road, a favourite trick was to come up behind a rival when he was pushing the food cart up the hill to the hospital and kick him in the rear for not bowing.

Sometimes through sheer mismanagement or ill-temper on the part of one of the Japanese, our meals would be held up for several hours. This was especially liable to happen when a very hostile person called Kobiyashi was in charge. None of us knew where we stood or what might happen next, but it was the men and women in charge of the two camps who bore the chief brunt of personal unpleasantness. The Japanese officials used to scream at them, stamp their feet, bang the tables with their fists and wave their hands about in paroxysms of rage. I was later told that this is quite uncharacteristic of their usual manner which is soft even to soapiness. It was probably put on in imitation of the more assertive ways of white people, especially Americans!

For some reason, the women in camp were never subjected to any special insult, in strong contrast to Japanese behaviour in conquered towns in China. The impression was that they had definite orders to avoid any incidents of this kind. We also gathered that on the whole, Western women were not very attractive to them. Some of the foreign women who were interned with us later were said to have been their "housekeepers" in Malaya and we regarded them as spies. A German-Swiss who was not interned became the mistress of one of the generals. She was ultimately killed in a motor accident near Johore, but according to another rumour the general in fact had got tired of her and had had her "taken for a ride". I had known her when I was a V.A.D. as she had attended some of the same nursing practices. She was bossy and domineering, always trying to dictate to the sister who was teaching us. It was not surprising that she bored a Japanese general.

For the first few months in camp, we were entirely supervised by Japanese. Later, Sikh guards were put in charge of the men's fatigues. Some of them were members of our own local police force and were as kind as they dared to be. One elderly man who had been severely beaten previously for indulgence to prisoners permitted me, at his own risk, to give coffee to the carpenters who were putting up shelves in my cell. Others were recruited from the dregs of the populace, cringing to the authorities and bullying the internees whenever possible, only anxious to curry favour with the Japanese by spying on prisoners or in any other way. All, indeed, were very frightened, with wives and families to maintain, and liable to beating and even beheading if their loyalty to the authorities was questioned.

In Changi, the women were confined to the gaol but the men were allowed out on various fatigues. They brought in firewood for the kitchens, grew vegetables on wasteland and went down to the sea to drag back carts full of water from which salt was extracted as there was a shortage of salt.

Our official camp shopping was done by permission of the Japanese officials, through Japanese dealers, both of whom made a huge rake-off on the prices. They never attempted to feed us adequately and after the Kempeitai took charge, they made it impossible for us to do much towards feeding ourselves. Our staple supplies were rice, the ration varying greatly from time to time, an insufficient quantity of vegetables, very little salt, and a ludicrously inadequate amount of oil. At Sime Road, we received supplies of *blachan* (mashed shrimp cake). It appeared to have decayed while drying in the sun, and the smell made Europeans want to vomit. It was however our only source of protein at that time, and the cooks in the men's camp were able to disguise it with curry powder to make it tolerable. They also supplied soya bean milk for the children.

Mr. Schweitzer, a Swiss, the International Red Cross representative, was never allowed to enter the camp, though after a time he was permitted to send in a few supplies of cigarettes, sweets, soap and talcum powder. He was not allowed to send food. Some people used the talcum powder for cooking. It had a sweetish queer taste and unless mixed with *kanji*, it set rather like cement, but it was something to eat for a change. We were not too badly off for soap. It may have been the Japanese dread for epidemics which made them give it to us fairly regularly.

Mr. Schweitzer once sent in some cotton material, four yards for every woman, and enough to make sheets, screens and curtains for the men's and women's hospitals which needed them badly. Otherwise the only clothing supplied to us was some second-hand things which were sent in once or twice, and a pair of knickers looted from Whiteaway's shop in Kuala Lumpur, which General Saito who was then in charge of enemy aliens presented to us in 1944. We called this gift "The General's Pants". By the end of internment, many people were barefooted and in rags. Material was very short in the whole country, the population outside being rationed at the rate of one yard of new material per head. Before the end of the War, some of the Japanese sentries themselves were in a patched and ragged state.

In Changi, parties of military, naval and civilian visitors often came to the camp during the rest hour on Sunday afternoons. We appeared to be a popular sight. We called these tours "Visiting the Zoo". The visitors were perfectly well-behaved but we disliked being disturbed and stared at. The women living on A-III, the lowest floor of the cells had a particularly trying time. They used to lie on their camp beds on the railed concrete space in the middle of their corridor, wearing nothing but brassieres and panties, half asleep in the heat. At the thud of army boots ascending the iron stairs, there was a shuffle and scuffle from A-III as the sleepers leapt from their beds and dived into their cells for shelter. This sometimes happened two or three times in the afternoon. It was not agreeable to be on show but sometimes it was quite amusing to watch unobserved the different types who came to look at us.

A party of German naval officers once came round and had the grace to look ashamed of themselves. Every now and again we had to prepare for a state inspection by "a very important official", and clear all our belongings off the railings and walls where they usually hung, and make the place unnaturally neat for his benefit. Two such inspections resulted in a temporary improvement in our diet. After the first, by a Japanese who was said to have been an ambassador in England, we were given a good meat stew at lunch-time for six weeks. After the second visit some time later by a man who was said to be the Emperor's brother and a representative of the International Red Cross, our food was increased.

We did not have much cause to love our Japanese guardians. They stole our Red Cross parcels. For part of the time they half starved us. They neither sent the majority of our letters home nor gave us all those which were addressed to us. The Kempeitai killed and tortured a number of our people and others died for want of easily procurable medicine, bad living conditions and lack of proper food. Nevertheless, after liberation, when we heard of the horrors of Belsen and the other German camps, those of us who retained any sense of proportion realised that we were probably the best internment camp in the world, apart from those for enemy aliens in England and the United States. In fact, a woman Red Cross representative who came to Sime Road and had visited many foreign camps told us that we were the best she had seen. The Japanese perpetrated many horrors in other prison camps and outside them, and upon the general public of the countries they captured. It is only fair to give them credit for refraining from committing as much evil as they easily might have done, and for the genuine efforts of some of them, at risk of their lives, at civilised behaviour, kindliness and humanity.

Interview

On 1 April 1943, a Senior Japanese officer interviewed Lady Thomas, wife of the British governor. The officer said that he had been in England and the United States of America but his English was rather defective. Also present at the interview were Lt. Suzuki, Mr. Tominaga, another Japanese officer and Dr. Cicely Williams, who recorded the interview.

Nipponese Officer (N.O.) You, Mrs. Thomas?

Lady Thomas   Yes.

N.O.   I come here special to see you.

Lady T.   That is very kind of you.

N.O.   You told them to hang out the white flag at Government House so Singapore had to surrender.

Lady T.   No, certainly not. I did not want to surrender.

N.O. (insisting) But you told them to hang out the flag at Government House.

Lady T.   Certainly not. Nothing of the sort. You have been misinformed.

N.O.   Then who surrendered? Your husband?

Lady T.   The military were in command. We had to do what they advised.

N.O.   Oh, so you did not surrender but Percival surrendered Singapore. Singapore—you know what that name means? Lion city …

Lady T.   Yes, the British lion, it means.

N.O.   Now you have lost it. It is no more British. It is now Syonan. The "shining" in the South, and after a little time it will become the "brilliance" in the South. Now it is no longer British—it is Nipponese.

Lady T.   Yes, temporarily.

N.O.   Temporarily?

Lady T   Yes, only temporarily.

N.O.   During the British regime Singapore was very dirty city.

Lady T   No, it was very clean.

N.O.   No, it was very dirty.

Lady T   As a matter of fact it had less epidemic disease than any other city in the East.

N.O.	It has no parks.
Lady T.	Oh, yes. It had the Botanical Gardens, and swimming baths, and many golf courses, and the park on East Coast Road, and all round MacRitchie Reservoir.
N.O.	You have children here?
Lady T.	No, none here. My daughter is in England, and my grandson.
N.O.	Oh, you do not like to be here. Here it is very tiresome.
Lady T.	Yes, very tiresome. No one likes to stay in prison.
N.O.	I think you stay here ten years. The food is very bad.
Lady T.	Yes, it is not all nice.
N.O.	You are very thin. How old are you?
Lady T.	I am 56. My husband is 63.
N.O.	You are very old and you are getting older every time. Where is your husband?
Lady T.	My husband was sent to Formosa. I asked to go with him. I was not allowed. Do you know Formosa?
N.O.	Yes.
Lady T.	Do you know how my husband is looked after? Is the food good?
N.O.	Yes.
Lady T.	Better than here?
N.O.	Yes.
Lady T.	What sort of house does he live in?
N.O.	I don't know.
Lady T.	What sort of place does he stay in?
N.O.	I don't know.
Lady T.	Really, don't you know that?
N.O.	You have been bombed?

Lady T.	Oh, yes, we were bombed.
N.O.	Government House was quite safe. Only the Chinese and poor people were bombed.
Lady T.	No, that is not at all true. Government House was bombed and shelled and badly damaged. Many of our people were killed.
N.O.	You ran away.
Lady T.	No, I did not run away. I stayed here. You see I am here now.
N.O.	Why did you stay here?
Lady T.	I wished to stay with my husband and my friends.
N.O.	Your friends are only Europeans?
Lady T.	Not at all. I have many friends who are Chinese, Indians and Malays.
N.O.	How long you stay here?
Lady T.	I have been here seven years. In seven years you make many friends. You get very fond of the place and people.
N.O.	You are connected with Churchill?
Lady T.	Well, not really connected. I admire him very much.
N.O.	You admired him? Churchill and Roosevelt are postponing the war. You know. They postpone the war. (Lady Thomas and myself both disclaimed being able to understand this. He meant "prolonging".)
N.O.	They postpone the war a hundred years. They all the time make preparations.
Myself	Yes, I am sure they are preparing quite a lot of things.
N.O.	You. You are a doctor?
Myself	Yes, I am a doctor.
N.O.	You have much work?

Myself	Yes, quite a lot.
N.O.	How many?
Myself	We have about 420 women and children in the Women's Camp.
N.O.	It is very bad for children in the prison.
Myself	It is, but we look after them very well.
N.O.	You know Mrs. Use?
Myself	No. No one of that name here.
N.O.	Mrs. Use. Mrs. Use. She is here. She come back.
Myself	(to the other Nipponese) Does he mean Lady Heath?
Lt. Suzuki	Ah, yes, Hease
Myself	She is really coming back?
Lt. Suzuki	Two or three days she will come back.

(It was then indicated that we could go.)

7 How to Run a Camp

Our internal organisation as a women's camp was not arrived at
without much confusion and bickering, and many false starts.
Eventually we were established with a Commandant, chosen at
elections held every three months, an Executive Committee of
five who were responsible for our dealings with the Japanese, and a
General Committee of twelve others. This seemed a large number of
officials to deal with the affairs of four or five hundred people but where
everything, including space, air and water, was very limited, a high
degree of organisation was necessary to ensure fairness of distribution
and of treatment, and a moderate degree of contentment. The whole
Committee met once a week to discuss camp affairs. Once a month,
there was a General Meeting of the entire camp which soon became
the curse of our lives.

Many of the women, including the Europeans, seemed to have
had no experience of working with others, of keeping to the point
in a discussion, or of any sort of responsibility. The result was that
the General Meeting rapidly degenerated into a series of prolonged
squabbles, and the more peace-loving members of the camp gradually
ceased to attend. Camp politics, that is to say energetic little intrigues

to get oneself or one's friends onto the Committee, became a major interest with a few people and a major nuisance to everyone else. In fact, the only benefit to the camp when the Kempeitai took charge was that, by forbidding people to meet in groups of more than four, they put an end to camp politics. The first Commandant, Dr. Hopkins, used to begin these meetings with a few remarks recalling to our memories the fact that, though prisoners of the Japanese, we were still members of a great Empire, and that the inevitable pettiness of our daily lives did not constitute the whole of the picture of which we formed a small part. Many of these addresses were stimulating and inspiring, but as time went on and people became more and more engulfed in the routine of our narrow lives, such considerations were forgotten. It was both comic and pathetic to hear women talking as though Winston Churchill's main preoccupation should be how to set us free.

If one were to believe the camp critics, all the women elected to the Executive Committee were as wicked as they were lazy and stupid. It was remarkable how each person began her public career in a haze of hope and glory and ended it in something like disgrace. It was partly that after a time, the internees became tired of even the most good-natured and efficient woman and longed for a change of personalities, any change, even one for the worse. The members of the Executive Committee were expected to perform miracles vis-à-vis the Japanese, that is, in "getting something" for the camp or for an individual. Failure was liable to provoke fierce resentment.

The Japanese rather liked fomenting trouble, and also to condescend, so they would sometimes grant favours to applicants who approached them personally when they were touring the gaol, something which they would peremptorily refuse to an official who saw them daily. At the same time (to make things more difficult), one of the rules which they were always emphasising was that they were only to be approached by a Committee member. The men, though they had their full share of "camp scandals", that is accusations of abuse of privileges and camp resources, much worse ones than ours, seemed to manage their "politics" better than we did. This was partly because their numbers were five or six times as great as ours so that the personal element counted for much less, and also because there were many more people among them accustomed to responsibility and organised work.

The Executive Committee consisted of the Commandant and her Deputy, the Camp Superintendent and her Deputy, and a member from the General Committee. The women of the General Committee were nicknamed "floorwalkers" because each floor of cells was under the management of two of them. A system of voting was worked out whereby women who did not live in cells but who camped in workshop-dormitories and alleyways were similarly represented. The floorwalkers had to distribute things sent by the Red Cross, sell sugar, sweets and bananas and other things when these were available through purchases made with camp funds, settle disputes between members of the same floor, arrange the work of each floor, deal as far as possible with theft from the cells, enforce the silence hour in the afternoon, and see that lights were put out at night at the required time. They had an arduous life and people's happiness depended very much on their efficiency, fairness and good temper. They were elected by the members of their respective floors.

We had other posts such as Storekeeper and Librarian. At one time, we were so overwhelmed with elections for an Entertainment Committee, a Housing Committee, a Committee of Child Welfare, as well as the usual Camp Committee, that we grew quite sick of the whole business. The Welfare Committee dealt partly with the organisation of games and other amenities for the children, but it was primarily necessitated by some shocking cases of cruelty among mothers and guardians of the children. Some of the mothers were of low mentality, and had very little self-control, and they could be exceedingly violent with their children. They beat them unmercifully with wooden sandals, or with a strap soaked in water to make it more cutting. One Eurasian baby of about eighteen months used to attend the crêche with weals on his body which lasted a week.

There was a good deal of opposition to the formation of this Committee, chiefly from the mothers concerned, backed up by some of the camp politicians who wanted the mothers' votes at the next camp elections, but it was finally formed through the determination of Dr. Patricia Elliott of St. Andrew's Mission Hospital. At a meeting of all the women which Dr. Elliott called independently of the Committee, it was decided by a large majority, which included many of the mothers themselves, that these cruelties must be stopped. A legal opinion from lawyers among the men, to the effect that cases of gross maltreatment could be punished under English law after liberation, gave the Committee strong support. After its formation, the worst cases of cruelty ceased.

Fights between women occurred occasionally, and ultimately the Japanese permitted us to punish these cases with a few days' solitary confinement. They mainly took place between the poorer class Eurasian women, though in one case, a Dutch woman and an Asian were involved. They stood in the office for some time calling each other "black bitch" and "white cow" before the officials could quieten them. There was always a certain amount of good-natured sympathy with these cases, since there were few internees who did not at some time feel a burning wish to clout somebody themselves.

The Housing Committee was formed in 1943 to deal with one of the most vexed questions in camp—the distribution of floor space.

This was one of the most important things in our lives and a tactful, sympathetic and fair handling of the problems made all the difference to happiness and comfort. The "space" was home. All personal possessions were kept in one's "space", and here only was it possible to retain even an illusion of privacy and independence. The amount and location of the "space", the personalities of one's neighbours and their idiosyncracies, or in the case of the cells, those of one's cellmate, made the whole difference between a life that was bearable and one that was intolerable. Real or fancied unfairness in the distribution of accommodation, the retention by a few people, mostly on medical grounds, of a cell to themselves when the rest had to share, or the possession of an especially comfortable corner in a dormitory roused extreme jealousy and resentment, complicated by the violent alliances and feuds which were inevitable in such a cramped existence. Under these conditions, it was almost impossible to settle housing problems peacefully and to the satisfaction of all concerned. The doctors had to fight very hard to secure proper treatment for sick women.

The Housing Committee instituted an arrangement of "rest cells" whereby the strain of sharing was relieved by splitting up cell partnerships for two months and giving each a private cell for that time. Complications sometimes arose at the end of the rest period when the partners refused to reunite. There was also a good deal of ill-feeling as to the way in which rest periods were allotted, while nothing could be done to relieve the strain of communal existence on those who lived in dormitories. Some people preferred the total lack of privacy of the dormitories, having an absolute horror of the cells. In the cells it was always possible, by an arrangement between cellmates, for each to obtain an hour of privacy in the cell during the day.

The difficulties of accommodation were increased as the Japanese sent fresh internees into the camp, sometimes in twos or threes, sometimes in quite large batches. Most of these new internees were Eurasians or foreign Europeans. There was a strong prejudice against foreigners among some Englishwomen, which made some of the newcomers' lives very unhappy, as they received all sorts of snubs and unkindness from their neighbours. In the spring of 1943, the Japanese brought about 100 Jews, mostly Asians, into the men's camp and put them into a room which abutted onto our Rose Garden which had been used as the Rice Store. It measured about 60 by 40 feet and contained one lavatory and one tap.

In December 1943 and January 1944, they brought in over 100 women and children to our camp. They were housed in the Printer's Workshop, the machinery and printing presses having been removed. The floor was spaced out equally. Screens were erected round two squatter lavatories. There was already one sink with one tap—the accommodation was complete. The new internees included Czechs, Poles, two German women, a French woman, a Belgian nun, some Englishwomen with Chinese husbands, many Eurasians and some Asians who could not speak a word of English. Among the latter were four Iraqi gypsy women and their children. They were very dirty but good-looking, very lively, independent, intelligent but thievish and wore ragged clothes.

They presented many problems to the nursing sisters. The youngest child, an enchanting curly-haired baby called Fatima, was quite unhousetrained and did her little duties about the prison when and where the fancy took her. She made friends with a little fair Eurasian girl of about the same age, and the two might be seen solemnly trotting up the concrete corridors hand in hand, the little Eurasian occasionally stopping to "dress" Fatima, whose one garment, a bright emerald-green nightgown devoid of buttons, was usually kilted very high or slipping off her brown shoulder. All the Iraqis were completely unselfconscious which was their great charm. Though usually pleasant to deal with, they were liable to fits of furious rage with one another—two had been wives of the same man and one was said to have poisoned him. One day, their floorwalker, a diminutive Czech, was summoned by some of her flock to deal with a row between these two. Seeing that one of them was flourishing a knife, she rushed forward and caught her by the wrist, to find herself confronted by the other brandishing a large glass bottle in a business-like fashion. No creatures more incongruous to a prison environment could have been found, and it was a mystery why the Japanese thought it necessary to intern them at all. In time, they grew sadly tamed.

The old internees' first feeling towards newcomers was one of pity. Later, this would be succeeded by resentment and envy at their having been left at large so long, and by jealousy of the equipment and tins of food which the lucky ones were able to bring with them. It took about a year for the new internees to be assimilated into the life of the camp. It was curious to see how their reactions to prison life were an exact repetition of what our own had been. They clamoured and protested against the inevitable, lamented, quarrelled, stole and grew bitter with one another, just as we had done. The old lags noted these kickings against the pricks with a mixture of amusement and sympathy and sometimes with irritation, knowing that they would settle down in time as they realised how unavailing all their protests were.

Thoughts in Changi Gaol

Poem written in August 1943 on being told that the Germans had hanged sixteen-year-old girls in the streets of Oslo for refusing to work in Germany.

It's true we are run by committee
Which give us a pain in the neck:
It's true and a trial and a pity
Our schoolgirl complexion's a wreck:
It's true if the foe's full of whiskey
We're apt to get slapped or be slanged,
But the girls of sixteen can be frisky—
They certainly haven't been hanged.

It's true that the food is repulsive
And quite insufficient as well:
If you speak to a man, all impulsive,
They'll possibly beat him to hell.
Our government may have rewarded
The prudence of those who escaped:
But dull though our life is and sordid
We certainly haven't been raped.

It's true that our nerves are in tatters,
Our tempers alarmingly frayed,
It also is true, if it matters,
We chanced all these things when we stayed.
It's true that we lie, steal and backbite,
That mostly our manners have fled,
It's true that we slander and catfight,
But still, all the same, we're not dead.

It's true when we get out of prison
We'll half of us land on the shelf:
The splendid new world that has risen
Won't offer much comfort or pelf.
Starvation and strikes for our suppers,
And slumps and revolts with our tea,
But even if down to our uppers
At least, oh, at least, we'll be free.

8 Work and Amusements

From the beginning the Japanese had ordered that everyone must work and be responsible for their own personal chores. There were also camp chores to be done. These jobs were many and varied. They included the serving of food, cleaning the drains, office work, nursing and cleaning in the hospital, cleaning of passages, stairs and lavatories, teaching and supervision of children, and gardening. The food servers came in for perennial criticism. The work required a certain amount of skill and judgement as the portion per person varied from day to day, but it also gave abundant opportunity for valuable "perks" and for favouring one's friends. Servers were sometimes unfair or very rude to people whom they disliked in the queue. Sometimes people in the queue were very rude to the servers.

The way the soup was served often caused a great deal of complaint. It was sent over in tubs and all the thick, solid vegetables sank to the bottom. Unless the servers kept on stirring, the first comers got a thin liquid while the later ones got a thick vegetable stew. When people got really hungry, differences like this caused very bitter feelings. The servers were under observation the whole time from hungry members of the queue. As time went on, the instinct to grab all one could for oneself, and to favour one's friends and those from whom some favour might be expected in return, became more and more universal.

In Changi, there was very fierce criticism of a special table where the food was kept hot for Committee members, doctors, and some nurses who could not get away from their work at meal times.

The cleaning of drains was always spoken of with much bitterness as representing the lowest depths of degradation, but in actual practice, some of the cleaners preferred it to any other work. It was performed alone in the cool of the morning. Hardworking sweepers took an interest in scrubbing off the green slime on the concrete daily, and prided themselves on the beautiful cleanliness of the section of drain under their care. These drains were intended only to carry off the heavy rainfall but they also carried a certain amount of rubbish. The worst rubbish came from the central yard where the Sikh guardroom was, but apart from this I never found much to sweep down my drains but red sand. At Sime Road, many of the drains were in a very dilapidated condition. Our brushes were also worn out and the Japanese either could not or would not replace them, and we had to do our best with bundles of bamboo twigs tied together, and by flinging down pails and pails of water to carry off the rubbish.

All the nursing duties in the hospital were done by about fifty trained English nursing sisters. Some had married and retired before the war but had returned to their work when there was a shortage of staff. They worked four hours a day, five days a week, taking their turn of night duty and extra, special nursing of dangerously ill or dying cases, while in the weeks intervening between their regular hospital duty, they took on camp chores. At one time, it was difficult to get volunteers to do the hospital laundry, a filthy job which included the dirty sheets of dysentery patients. The aged, the sick, the infirm, the children, and the mothers with families to look after were all exempted from the more exacting camp chores. But in 1944, when the Japanese began to pay the camp workers, and in 1945, when they gave them half a pint of rice-porridge (*kanji*) extra per day, it was remarkable to see a number of people who had previously been unable to do any work come eagerly forward demanding to be given their share.

Under the supervision of two ex-hospital matrons, Miss Simmonds and Mrs. Nairn, the more delicate women took over the camp sewing. Very weird and wonderful feats of patchwork and adaptation were accomplished by these ladies whose camp nickname was "The Sew-Sews". Their ingenuity seemed to increase as garments decreased, and I believe they found a positive pleasure in creating something out of next to nothing.

There was a perennial shortage of V.A.Ds, a hard job which carried no perks. They did the nursing and cleaning on the Convalescent Verandah, in the Sanatorium and in the Infirm Ladies' Annexe, working four-hourly shifts on alternate weeks. The nursing facilities on the Verandah were ingenious devices contrived by the camp workmen. The patients were protected from storms by an arrangement of bamboo blinds called "chicks", and by pieces of mackintosh. The concrete drain ran along the edge of the verandah and great agility was required in negotiating this hazard, especially when laden with trays of food, and particularly on wet days when everything was slippery with rain. When the storms really blew, the V.A.D. on duty flew round like a lunatic, letting down chicks and making them fast with tent pegs and pieces of string, while sheets of rain drove inwards on the wings of the hurricane. Any special cooking for the patients was done on open wood fires, in competition with the rest of the camp who would be trying to stew a curry, toast their bun, or boil water for tea. Later on, Dr. Worth got hold of an electric heater for the Sanatorium as well as a dilapidated electric stove for the Infirm Ladies' Annexe. The latter was a boon to half the camp as anybody might use it, provided the infirm ladies' cooking was given priority. Patients hospitalised on the verandah benefitted in health and it was considered a great privilege—probably favouritism—to be given a bed there.

In January 1944, the Japanese announced that we would be paid for camp work at the rate of 25 cents a day, irrespective of the type of work done or the time taken. Thus, a full-time office job and skilled medical nursing work received the same pay as was given for twenty minutes spent sweeping a corridor. This obviated a great many quarrels. We had to sign a receipt for a year to come, which sadly depressed the ever-hopefuls whose spirits were buoyed by the conviction that repatriation was never more than three weeks ahead. Personally, after the shock of a second Christmas as a prisoner, a possibility which I had never contemplated even in my most depressed moments, I settled down to a conviction of "certainly two, possibly four more years". This was a gloomy prospect but preferable to the trials of optimism continually disappointed, and it made one feel that the actual remaining period of about twenty months was a fortunate let-off.

We needed a Fatigue Officer to organise the camp work, to see that it was distributed as fairly as possible and that every job was done somehow. As can be imagined, it was not an easy post. One of the best Fatigue Officers was Kathleen Toussaint, a young Eurasian woman who was both efficient and tactful.

Though people naturally grumbled a good deal at the rough and uncongenial work we had to do, it was not too much for us. Although it was so different from anything done by Europeans in the East before, it did us no harm. When it was too much, this was not due to the character of the work itself but to the lack of proper food, and to the deep depression and listlessness arising from the circumstances in which we lived. Most people realised after a time that it was better to have some definite job, however trifling, than to do nothing at all. Those who worked actually benefitted in health and spirits, and the consciousness of contributing something to the good of the community helped to maintain self-respect under living conditions which were in many ways very degrading. The best off were those doing medical and administrative work since, however unpleasant might be the friction and criticism which it often entailed, it was positive and constructive and gave mental interest as well as physical occupation.

Boredom and listlessness were two great problems. I think this may be inevitable in any form of prison life, especially if it lasts long, such an existence being so painfully unreal and aimless. In Singapore, we were completely cut off from the educational facilities which were available to the P.O.W. camps in Germany, where men were able to pass standard examinations in such subjects as law and medicine, as well as in typing, shorthand and languages. Some people had brought a few books with them, and after a few months, the Japanese allowed us to collect a good general library from the libraries in Singapore. This was a great blessing to everyone. However, we never had the reference books necessary for any particular course of study, test books of any sort were very few, and also there were not many women among us capable of giving classes to adults.

Few people realise what books mean to prisoners. Only through books was it possible to leave the gaol and walk in a normal world again, coming back strengthened and refreshed. Among the many books I read, there were three which I read three or four times though possibly in ordinary life I might not have read them at all. In Changi, I read them because they took me out into the open air, and the natural world of trees, hills and wild creatures. Through one, *Lagooned in the Virgin Islands*, I entered a world of palm trees and sea, full of whispering sounds and sunlight glinting on moving water. With the other two, both of them cowboy stories, *Forlorn River* by Zane Gray, and *Hopalong Cassidy Returns*, I went out to huge bare plains, empty and peaceful under a vast sky, bordered with distant green mountains where wild horses and cattle grazed, and where the few human beings were all part of the sunlit open spaces.

I was able to read some books on religion and philosophy, reading which needs concentration and thought and for which ordinary life gives little opportunity. This reading included a large part of the Bible. I had a copy I had looted from someone's abandoned luggage in Fullerton Building. I also read *Buddhism* by Alexandra David Neal; *Confucius* by Alfred Doeblin, *The Golden Mean of Confucius*, and several books by Lin Yutang. From *My Country and My People*, I copied verses of Chinese poetry composed many centuries ago. On all these books I made copious notes which I still have. I considered becoming a Buddhist but its view of human existence seemed to me too dark.

"Life is bad," I thought, "but it is not as bad as that," and I remained a Christian; but I made notes direct from the Buddhist Scriptures which I still re-read from time to time, finding their different outlook profoundly illuminating and inspiring.

"All beings long for happiness: therefore extend your compassion to all" (Mahavanda). *All beings*—not only man. "Whatever your suffering, do not wound another" (Udanavarga), and many more. Phrases like these if taken seriously can transform our approach to life, even though we may not always live up to them.

The philosophy I read included Plato's *Republic*. I had read this before, but the translation we had in Camp included a passage which I learnt by heart and have never forgotten: "To lie, and to be the victim of a lie: to be ignorant in the soul concerning reality, to hold and possess falsehood there: that is the last thing any man would desire." It is Socrates speaking, dealing as always with what is fundamental, and making so much subsequent philosophising look thin and poor.

I read Chaucer's translation of Boethius and found a sentence I liked very much, heartening as it was in our circumstances. "Hast thou ever any commandment over a free courage?", "courage" being used in the 14th century sense of "mind" or "spirit". I remembered too many lines from T.S. Elliot's poem *Ash Wednesday* which I often repeated to myself:

> Teach us to care and not to care
> Teach us to sit still.

The travels of Freya Stark, the detective stories of Dorothy Sayers, and many other novels, books and poetry were among my reading.

Qualified teachers conducted physical culture and dancing classes as well as verse-speaking, and lectures on medicine and first aid. A particularly spirited effort was the teaching of Italian by Mrs. del Tufo, an elderly crippled lady who lived in the Infirm Ladies' Annexe. She had left Italy at the age of twelve, but she succeeded in reviving her memories of the language so thoroughly as to be able to give lessons to several classes of pupils, at first without even the help of a grammar book. The German wife of an English internee had a class of pupils throughout internment, and a frail old Belgian nun, Mother St. Cyr, the former Reverend Mother of a Roman Catholic Convent in Malacca, gave many people lessons in French.

An artist, Mrs. Angela Bateman, very delicate and no longer young, was indefatigably kind in giving lessons and private help to a group of very keen pupils whenever she was well enough. This class had the greatest difficulty in getting materials. The men got hold of some good drawing paper which they very kindly sent to Mrs. Bateman who distributed it among the class. We also used writing paper, foolscap, the backs of old prison memoranda found in the office, packing paper and anything else we could get hold of. The paints we managed to obtain were mostly of very poor quality and faded badly. At one time we were so short of supplies that I tried the experiment of painting with a mixture of red earth and water, which gave results rather like red chalk. A mixture of water and soot off the cooking pots was less successful as the soot was too gummy.

A few months after we were first interned, a small "Malayan Reconstruction Circle" was started by a few friends, headed by Dr. Cicely Williams and Mrs. de Moubray. It began by discussing problems relating to education and the Malayan Medical Service, and then digressed to such various topics as chicken-farming and Bertrand Russell's *Conquest of Happiness*. These discussions helped to create a happier outlook by taking attention away from our immediate dreary problems and focussing it on matters of wider and more impersonal interest.

Russell's book contained an encouraging passage in praise of boredom as affording a period for the mind to lie fallow and refresh itself for new and more important work. Since we were often bored in Camp, I found this remark very valuable and took much comfort from it, but after I came home I heard the great philosopher describing the boredom of life in the country in most disparaging terms. I thought, "This man is inconsistent!", and I lost much of my respect for the thoughts of Bertrand Russell.

With the permission of the Japanese, concerts were occasionally held, and the women were twice allowed to attend the entertainment given by the men in the central yard. The Japanese also used to attend these concerts and seemed to enjoy them very much, though a good many of the jokes about prison life must have passed over their heads or they would have taken exception to them. They did not appreciate concerts of classical music, though these were enjoyed by the camp as they would probably never have been in normal times. Comparatively unmusical people like myself looked forward eagerly to them, and I developed a sort of craving for the music of Bach and Beethoven. There was something in our lives which made us long for the disciplined and impersonal harmony of great music. The men also had a very good choir. They were allowed to sing carols to us on Christmas eve and occasionally to give concerts at other times, and they had some excellent pianists. It was very difficult for these pianists to keep up their playing, because the sound of practising got so much on people's nerves that it was almost entirely forbidden.

There was not much music in the women's camp because although we had a piano, there was nowhere suitable to play it. It was kept in the Carpenter's Shop where most of the camp's noisiest activities also took place—school drill and singing games, the Sew-Sews complete with sewing machines, the daily queue for the library, and the washing of clothes. The piano as an instrument was inaudible and merely added extra noise to the general discord, but there was nowhere else to keep it. We had one first-rate pianist but unfortunately the timetable for the piano-users was arranged in such a way that it was practically impossible ever to hear her play. A former Russian opera singer gave singing lessons and developed a really beautiful voice in one young Eurasian singer, but owing to the general objection the classes died out.

An immense addition to our comforts and interests occurred during the summer of 1942 when Mrs. Mulvaney, the wife of a Canadian P.O.W., obtained permission from the Japanese to go shopping in the town and buy food, clothing and other articles for re-sale in the camp. The excitement of these periodic shopping days was tremendous and gave an enormous stimulus to our lives. While they lasted, they gave us one of the greatest privileges we ever enjoyed. Anxiety about the future could be allayed by buying tinned foods as a reserve for emergencies, deficient or almost non-existent wardrobes could be replenished, and people were also able to buy such things as drawing materials, playing cards, sewing and embroidery kit, writing paper and ink, without which many of our occupations and classes would have been out of the question.

Mrs. Mulvaney also helped women who were short of money by selling for them any odds and ends which they liked to part with. As a businesswoman she had one great weakness, which was that she could not keep accounts. Probably she did not see any necessity for them. Her harum-scarum system or total want of system caused much criticism in the camp, but the most expert assistance could not tame her. Of her personal generosity there could be no doubt. At Sime Road, she was in hospital for a time and her friends took charge of her baggage for her. In it they found a great number of articles which she had undertaken to sell for needy internees and which, when she could not find a buyer, she had quietly bought with her own money at the seller's price. At the time she was herself quite short of money and the articles were of no use to her. Those who had given her the things to sell had no idea of what she had done to help them.

For a few months during the 1943, we had lectures who conducted courses on astronomy, drawing, Bible study, and other subjects. Once a month, there was a Question Hour when speakers from the men's camp were given ten minutes each to reply to enquiries on different subjects sent beforehand by the women. Some of these discourses were very lively and amusing. One short talk, in response to a question about the difference between slander and libel and their possible legal consequences, had the unlooked-for result of frightening the more extravagant gossips into an unwonted restraint which lasted for several months.

Gossip was continuous and incredibly petty. It was a hunt for sensation pure and simple, a vent for all the accumulated boredom and frustration of life. In both camps, people came to feel like insects pinned to a dissecting-board. The most trivial events of daily life were observed, commented on, discussed, chewed over, interpreted and misinterpreted, till no one could change the corner in which they ate their meals, lie down to rest with a backache, or say good-morning to a friend without causing a sensation. It was like being continually buzzed over by a crowd of bluebottles.

In the gaol, one of our great problems was how to get enough fresh air. Many people used to take their camp beds into the compounds at night and sleep out of doors in spite of the frequent storms. Many others took chairs and stools and sat talking in the compounds for an hour or so after lights out. The serene atmosphere of night was as lovely in gaol as it is anywhere else—perhaps by contrast with our daylight surroundings it was more lovely.

Voices were softened, moonlight and starlight cast a charm over the prison walls, and shadows altered the familiar shapes and hid a multitude of sordid, makeshift ugliness. Year by year the remote, impersonal stars followed their paths over the sky, and our minds felt liberated in watching them. If the Japanese had realised how much we loved this sitting-out at night, they would probably have forbidden it or interfered to spoil it in some way, as they sometimes interfered with our gardening, smoking and other harmless pleasures.

In the gaol there was little scope for gardening. The compounds when we arrived were bare except for coarse grass and gravel and we had to allot a good deal of space for drying clothes and airing bedding, as well as giving up one exercise yard to the children, so that there was not much room left for gardens. Marvellous results were achieved along the edges of banks and drains and in waste corners.

Tropical plants matured very rapidly, and papaya trees planted from seed bore fruit within a year if they were well manured. My cellmate, Margaret Young, planted papaya seeds along the edge of a drain in "A" Compound soon after our arrival in gaol. Twelve months later we had fruit from them.

Our only manure was vegetable compost and human urine, both of which gave excellent results if used in sufficient quantities. The soil was very poor, a compound of laterite and clay. After the rain, it was a sticky mass and practically unworkable, while a few days' drought set it like a brick. In spite of these drawbacks, the camp gardeners grew a few vegetables, chiefly mint and beans, and there were many narrow borders of shrubs and flowers, some of whose leaves could be picked and eaten as salad. One of the loveliest sights was the leaves of the papaya trees which, as they faded, first turned pale yellow, then deep gold, and finally a vivid rusty brown. The papaya tree has a long slender stem with a crown of long-staked leaves growing out of it at the top. It has no branches and is not really a tree at all but an overgrown plant, relic of primeval times. The male papaya has festoons of cream-coloured flowers with a very sweet scent but is barren of fruit.

In one corner of "A" Compound, the gardeners grew a big clump of sugarcane, twelve feet high, and it was pleasant to sit and read under the shade of its long, rustling streamers. Near the sugarcane was a plant called Japanese convolvulus with a big fragile blossoms of the palest mauve. It climbed over some bamboo poles which surrounded a row of latrine boreholes that the Japanese had dug in a panic, after the water supply once failed for twenty-four hours. They were never used and the place was taken over by the gardeners as a sort of open-air potting shed, and was another pleasant spot in which to read.

Close by ran one of the main camp drains, through which a stream of running water was always maintained to keep it sweet. The water rushed in a noisy little cascade through a trap which led the drain under the wall into the men's adjacent compound. Sometimes it was possible to imagine one was listening to a bubbling stream running through a wood in England.

There was a small piece of woodland near my home in the Cotswold hills of which the running water especially reminded me. This wood offered one of the most beautiful vistas of spring that one could wish to discover, and to be reminded of it in Changi Gaol was no small thing. I had always thought of it in terms of some lines from a poem by Robin Flower:

> It was the Fairy Wood:
> We called it so, for all we knew of good
> And beautiful and beyond belief remote
> Dwelt in those brakes of bracken and bright fern.

There was no bracken nor much fern in my little wood, but the poetry expressed the spirit which filled it. It had no tall trees; it was a coppice wood, that is, its trees were cut down to the ground every six or seven years to make hurdles for use on the farm, so they grew more like tall bushes and were never big enough to keep the sun off the plants growing round them. Because of this, the wood was full of sunlight and full of wild flowers, all the flowers of spring it seemed to me: primroses on a certain bank, bluebells everywhere, blue dog violets most lovely though scentless, thin-stemmed buttercups, even cowslips flourishing in some places and, most wonderful of all, wind-flowers, the delicate, graceful wood anemone of Greek legend, which grew nowhere else in our neighbourhood. Through it all ran a little stream, tinkling with a small musical sound over pebbles and moss, its ripples catching the sunlight as they ran, with a few plants of brilliant golden kingcups growing near. The stream left the wood to run through a steeply sloping meadow to join a larger one which had cut itself a deep path under tall trees and thorn bushes whose roots showed along the banks. In one place the water plunged in a noisy cascade two feet down to where its bed ran lower, with the spreading branches of trees leaning overhead. The water running from our "A" Compound drain reminded me of my English home.

I used to go very early in the morning to look at the Japanese creeper, whose flowers were at their loveliest before the sun was properly up, seeming to lose their peculiar, ethereal quality in the full glare of day. The grimness of the building and its prison atmosphere were so softened by the beauty of these growing things that the Japanese became angry, and one day ordered all the flowers to be pulled up and vegetables to be planted in their places. However, the flowers were mostly growing in places where vegetable cultivation was impossible, and this order was discreetly ignored. Nearly everybody grew mint which flourished in all sorts of odd containers, including an old tin hat, and was even grown inside the cells.

A few people kept pets. These included some dogs which had been brought with us, while others arrived on their own, and cats as usual turned up from nowhere. A small boy brought in his parrot, and a woman adopted a hen and some sparrows. The hen distinguished itself by providing eggs for the sick when other supplies were unavailable. Many people objected to the pets on the ground that they were dirty, but they gave such pleasure to so many people, besides lending a more normal atmosphere to the prison, that it seemed wrong to get rid of them. The Japanese on two occasions decided that there were too many dogs in the camp and had some shot.

The women had a newspaper called *Pow-Wow*, run by Mrs. Freddy Bloom, which was published every week till the coming of the Kempeitai. It contained short stories, articles, drawings, verse and items of camp news and gossip. One feature was a series of camp caricatures by Miss Parfitt. My own contribution was a humorous weekly commentary on camp affairs called "My Stars", under the signature of "The Old Squaw", a witch-like character domiciled in some unspecified corner of the camp. Many people decided that I could not be the author because I had not enough brains. A specimen of some articles from *Pow-Wow* may be found at the end of this book.

There were many clergy of all denominations in the men's camp but we were not allowed regular services until early in 1943. They were discontinued again when the Kempeitai took charge. In Sime Road, they were once more allowed, and the Bishop of Singapore was permitted to give addresses and advice on Saturday afternoons, when the Roman Catholic clergy also came over to hear confessions. Baptisms and confirmations were held during internment. The clergy were allowed to go out to Bidadari Cemetery to conduct the funeral services of internees who died in camp.

It was very difficult to get permission to visit sick or dying relatives in the opposite camp or in the Miyako Hospital. On this point the Japanese were extremely hard. Our death rate in both camps was not abnormally high, though many deaths were preventable, and except for some tuberculosis, diabetic and tropical typhus cases, the deaths occurred almost entirely among the aged. The most blameable of preventable deaths were those caused by lack of insulin which could easily have been supplied. All our diabetics died, the worst case being that of a young civil servant who lived to within a few months of our release. Not long after his death, the Japanese, who had refused to get us insulin earlier, brought some into the camp but he was the last of the diabetics and the supply was then useless. There were two suicides in the men's camp, where the overcrowding was much worse than in ours, and there were cases of mental breakdown in both camps.

About twenty babies were born during internment, all of mothers who had come in already pregnant. At first, the expectant mothers were sent to Kandang Kerbau Maternity Hospital for their confinements, but later this was stopped and the births took place in our own hospital. Dr. Smallwood acted as obstetrician. All the mothers and babies did very well.

Dysentery and other cases, including major operations, were sent to Miyako until early in 1943 when the Japanese refused to permit patients to be sent out, after which these cases too had to be treated in camp. I was sent to Miyako Hospital with mild dysentery, and as my place in the ward was not wanted for anyone else, I stayed there for six weeks, by the kindness of Dr. Balhatchet, the Eurasian Chief Medical Officer, on the plea that I needed dental attention. A stay in the Miyako Hospital provided a most welcome holiday from the camp. The Bishop, Padre Adams and Padre Hayter were regular visitors, bringing us news of the country and friends as well as presents of food and books. The hospital diet was very poor, so bad that a small allowance to patients to buy food was made from the camp funds. Hawkers who sold eggs, biscuits and fruit were permitted to come into the wards each day, while a hospital shop was run by Choy Koon Heng and his wife, Elizabeth, whose real intention was to send help to the internees. Innumerable men and women benefitted from the kindness and great courage of these two, and they paid very heavily for their goodness to us when the Kempeitai took over.

Many of the nurses also took great risks in showing kindness to internee patients. After I had got over my dysentery, an Arab girl, Jessie Artoon, used to send me presents of vermicelli, fried meat and tomatoes or some similar luxury nearly every evening from the hospital tuckshop. Such friendliness to the internees was liable to the heaviest punishments. Half our ward was occupied by some old Japanese women, retired prostitutes and amahs, who were liable to report everything that happened. Screens divided their portion of the ward from our half, but they managed to see most of what went on, and once got a nurse into trouble when she was accused of giving more attention to internee patients than to themselves.

In the early days of internment, men and women patients had been allowed to visit each other's wards quite freely, but when I went there this had been altered and men and women were kept strictly separated. The men and women doctors coming out from camp with the ambulance were allowed to visit all the internees' wards, and they took messages to and fro and gave news of friends. The English doctors who were still working at Miyako did as much to help us as they could, but they too were under very close observation. Dr. Williamson, the eye specialist, often came up for a surreptitious chat with the internees in the evening.

Within the gaol, the Japanese at first tried to keep the men and women entirely separate, except for necessary fatigue duties carried out in our camp by the men. Later, they gave permission for a certain amount of dental treatment and for some of the men doctors to come over for special consultations. Patients were also sent to the men's camp for operations, returning to our camp as soon as the operation was over. We were indebted to the men's camp for their invaluable help, since our own camp consisted largely of women with no special technical training of any kind.

We started off with about fifty children. Through births and the arrival of new internees, their number had increased to eighty when we left for Sime Road. After the influx of internees there in March 1945, it rose to about three hundred. The boys over ten were supposed to be sent to the men's camp but some anxious mothers succeeded in evading this rule for some time. Among the men were highly skilled chemists, engineers, electricians and technicians who were extraordinarily ingenious in inventing substitutes and contrivances. One of their inventions was spectacle frames made out of old tooth brush handles, which were excellent, though the wearer of a bright blue or scarlet frame was apt to feel self-conscious at first.

Quite early in internment, we were allowed to go to the sea once a month to bathe, the men and women going on different days appointed by the Japanese. The bath was allowed because the seawater was supposed to be good for health. It was almost the only concession which the Japanese initiated of their own accord. The expedition was stimulating and good fun in a variety of ways, especially for the women. Some of the men were allowed outside the gaol daily on various fatigues, but for a long time this sea bath was the only chance the women had to get beyond the walls. Not everyone went, partly because the Japanese usually kept us waiting in the sun for half an hour or so before starting—to show off, we supposed.

We were accompanied by sentries, sometimes Japanese, sometimes Sikhs, who were not unpleasant or unduly obtrusive. People usually came back laden with flowers and cuttings from shrubs growing in abandoned gardens along the cliffs. We undressed in a partly ruined house. It stood near a rubber plantation in which there were old shelter pits for English guns with a concrete gunpost near the shore, while in the sea were the remains of barbed wire entanglements put up to greet the enemy who never came by sea. On the way home, we picked up the coarse pottery cups which were used in tapping the latex in the plantation. We found them useful as food containers.

Once, on our way to the sea, we passed a house where local girls had been collected for the entertainment of Japanese officers. They were Malays, and were dressed in *bajus* (jackets) of coarse white lace and gaudy *sarongs*. They were wandering about in the small garden and they looked at us with mechanical smiles and an expression of blank misery in their eyes. The Japanese called such girls "comfort girls". They had been forcibly recruited and the house was a brothel.

When Mr. Naito was in charge, he allowed the men and women to walk outside the camp on alternate evenings. Barbed wire was erected around an area of waste ground, which the men were turning into a vegetable garden, and here we walked, sewed, or played bridge. The main road ran quite close to the fence and lorries carrying coolies, Japanese troops, and sometimes our own P.O.W. could be seen passing. Children were allowed out every evening and some of the men made a hobby of taking the babies for an airing. Sometimes the ungrateful babies would cry for no obvious reason, which greatly perplexed their nurses. My first walk under these circumstances was an extraordinary experience. I went out alone with a friend, most people having stayed behind to hear a lecture first. To walk quietly out of the gate unaccompanied by sentries and not in a crowd made us both grow silent, it was such a normal thing to do and yet so strange. There was a peculiar sensation in my eyes as they took in the unaccustomed distances and the variety and greenness of the landscape. This moment was more full of emotion, there was an acuter consciousness of the contrast between imprisonment and liberty than at any other time of internment. Soon after Mr. Tominaga took over from Mr. Naito, these walks were completely stopped, and the women were confined to the gaol until the move to Sime Road about ten months later.

One of the things to which a prisoner looks forward most is the arrival of letters from home, but whether through the fault of the Japanese or not, we did not receive these as often as we should. Sometimes we were told that 20,000 letters had arrived in the camp but after months of delay, only 8,000 were distributed. What happened to the rest, whether they were sent to P.O.W. camps or whether they were our own and the censors could not be bothered to deal with them, we were never told. We were only allowed to send five postcards and three radio messages during the whole three and a half years of internment, and many of these never arrived. One plane carrying our mail was shot down over the Irish Sea. My family only received one letter and one radio message from me. Not till Christmas 1943, after two years of internment, did they know that I was still alive. The names of prisoners were not broadcast soon after capitulation because of inefficiency, partly to laziness and indifference, and partly to unkindness. Some Japanese appeared to think comparatively little of the claims of family affection. One important officer told us, "Why do you make so much fuss about your families? You must be patient. It is eight years since I have seen my family."

Very soon after internment, the men constructed two receiving sets on which they received up-to-date British Broadcasting Corporation news which was disseminated in the two camps. Along with the news, many wild rumours went round. I have no idea how many times Germany "collapsed" before its actual end. For some months, we were also allowed to have the *Straits Times* newspaper, renamed *Syonan Shimbun* but still printed in English. This gave us little news of the war in Europe and only garbled, imperfect accounts of the situation in the East, but still it was something. It told us a good deal about what was happening under Japanese rule in Malaya. By reading between the lines, it was possible to form some idea of affairs in the world outside.

Although many women had relatives, husbands and friends in the men's camp, we had been interned for fifteen months before regular official meetings of relatives were allowed. Each Christmas, the women were allowed to invite a limited number of guests for an hour or two.

In the spring of 1943, a fair was held to get money to buy ducks and other animals to start a camp farm. This was under the benevolent rule of Mr. Naito. The men put up booths in one of our yards where coconut shies and other entertainment took place, and packets of salt, curry puffs, fruit, and other delicacies were for sale. The fair did not make much money but it was a wonderful change.

There was also a postal service between the two camps which was subject to censorship by the Japanese. As some of the women were very reckless in the items of gossip and rumour which they included in these letters, we had to elect four women censors to read them before they were handed to the Japanese Office. Such remarks as "I saw So-and-So over here with the plumbers this morning and he told me that you badly need a new pair of shorts" or "I felt so much cheered up after hearing the wonderful news about Libya" were liable to get the whole camp into trouble and lead to the stoppage of the postal service altogether. Nevertheless, some women were very angry at the idea of their letters being read by other internees. There was also a parcel service between the two camps through which the women sent cooked food over to the men. The men sent home-grown vegetables to their female friends, and books, clothes for mending, valuable empty tins, bottles and other objects were exchanged.

There were also many unofficial channels of communication between the two camps. Very private letters, which the censors could not be permitted to see, were slipped under doors or thrown over the compound walls at night. Under the cover of darkness, romantic conversations took place head-downwards through a drain which ran under the wall between the two camps. These interludes were made more exciting still by the possibility of being caught by prowling sentries armed with torches, or of being reported by another internee out of spite. The weekly official meetings were first allowed for families, and then for different categories of relations, until at last the expression "approved relatives" had been extended to cover almost every conceivable link. Thanks to both genuine and faked relationships, the latter being known as "Changi cousins", the great majority of the women obtained the privilege of these weekly meetings. They were held in our Rose Garden.

The men poured in from the central yard carrying mugs and stools and all looking as spruce as possible for the occasion. They had exchanged their habitual pair of ragged shorts or loincloth for clean and tidy if much-patched garments, stockings and shoes. The women, resplendent in lipstick and clean "best" clothes, carefully saved for meetings and for the great day of liberation, awaited them in the shade of the prison wall. They brought with them coffee or tea in tin cans. During the few months of 1943 when we could buy extra flour, fruit and vegetables in the camp, there were also cakes, puddings and biscuits made of pounded rice and flavoured with coconut or ginger, salads, and sometimes sago puddings dyed an elegant shade of blue with the clitoria blossoms.

It was a great comfort to our feelings to be able to iron our clothes, which we were able to do as a number of people had brought electric irons in with them. For no particular reason, after Mr. Tominaga became the head of the camp in 1943, the Japanese suddenly took away all our electrical appliances except those in the hospitals. Dr. Worth, however, ingeniously got some of the irons restored to us by drawing the attention of the Japanese to an increase in skin complaints, and urging the valuable germ-destroying effects of hot irons on clothing.

When we were first interned, a fatigue of men came over daily to take away and empty our camp dustbins. As this fatigue was mainly composed of husbands, it was always followed by a crowd of anxious and affectionate wives, all smartened up in their best, and quite reckless of the no-communication order. The attitude of the sentries in charge of the fatigue varied greatly. One man once went and fetched a wife whose husband was over on a working-party, and leaving them together in a quiet corner of a passage turned away saying, "Now you kiss him."

This attitude could by no means be depended on, and exasperated sentries would sometimes slap the faces of women who were too obtrusive. Finally the Japanese, finding it impossible to control the wives, forbade the men to fetch the dustbins at all and said the women must carry them themselves. This threatened to produce a camp crisis of the first magnitude, since the wives now declared they were too weak to carry heavy dustbins, and the spinsters and widows, who were already doing most of the camp work, said the wives had brought the situation on themselves and they were not going to carry dustbins either.

I do not know whose brain devised the brilliant solution which was finally arrived at, but it was arranged with the Japanese that the women should carry the dustbins into the central courtyard and there hand them over to the men for disposal outside the walls. Privately, the officials of the two camps decided that the wives should carry the dustbins and the husbands receive them. As soon as this was settled there was an overwhelming rush to get places on the dustbin fatigue. Extra dustbins had to be found to make up the numbers, and even so a roster had to be most carefully compiled so that all should get their fair turn. Each day, at about 10.30 a.m., one might see a stream of fortunate women, spruced in their best, marching solemnly in pairs up the passage to the central court, each grasping one handle of a dustbin.

The fatigue was always a source of great annoyance to the Japanese because of the unbreakable spirit of some of the wives, who persisted in waving, smiling and occasionally even speaking to their spouses.

A sentry, who was always very strict as he was more or less under observation from his own guardroom, was posted at the doorway of our quarters where the dustbins were handed over. Poor Miss Foss, a kind-hearted spinster, who was in charge of the Dustbin Parade, stood near him in a state of perpetual agitation for fear one of her charges should get beaten up, or that she should get beaten up too.

It never occurred to the Japanese to examine the contents of the dustbins, but had they done so they could have greatly reduced the numbers on parade, the bins being frequently less than half full as there was really not enough rubbish to go round. When I was convalescent after illness, and engaged in the light work of clearing up litter, I earned torrents of gratitude from a Eurasian internee by specially preserving all the choicest and bulkiest bits of rubbish for her bins.

Agony Column

Can I bear it any longer,
Queues and concrete, dust and noise?
Chill distance is growing stronger
Even for our so-called joys.
Mince at lunch no longer thrills me,
Eggs at supper leave me cold,
And it very nearly kills me
When the cigarettes are sold.

Sitting like a lonely pigeon,
Wondering how to charm the time—
Shall I learn a new religion?
Shall I start a life of crime?

Tunnel under the foundations?
That would take a year or two!
Reconstruct the League of Nations?
Start a private insect zoo?

Shall I join the busy bobbies,
Changi's gifted C.I.D.,
Poking into people's hobbies,
Counting buns and cups of tea?
Shall I loose my inhibitions?
Shall I take to sweeping drains?
Send round 'news' in new editons?
Date with other women's swains?

No, I will not: there's a limit.
No more evils will I choose:
Thus to fill my cup and brim it
Frankly, flatly, I refuse.
There's one certain way to banish
All the plagues at one full sweep:
Walls and women! Presto! Vanish!
Come what may I still can sleep.

Note: C.I.D. stands for Criminal Investigation Department

$\mathcal{9}$ Double Tenth

Soon after the beginning of internment, we began to receive news from the British Broadcasting Corporation on two wireless sets secretly made and operated by the men. This news was at first disseminated by word of mouth but later typed news-sheets were circulated in both camps. For the first sixteen months, the heads of the women's camp refused to distribute the typed sheets, though they were always ready to pass on the news orally. This distribution of type-written news was a piece of recklessness for which all concerned afterwards paid very dearly. It was especially reckless in the women's camp, where a very mixed Asian element was in the majority and included a number of women who were partly Japanese. We also had wild rumours, varying from American landings up and down both coasts of Malaya, to the date of repatriation, the exact day being foretold at least a hundred times, each time differently.

By our contacts with the town through the expeditions of the ambulance and the supply lorries, we got a good deal of information about conditions in Singapore. These were supplemented from time to time by the accounts given by fresh internees, Europeans and Eurasians, whom the Japanese were crowding into the prison. Sometimes we received radio news from persons outside the camp who passed on their information to those on the ambulance or to men working on the outside fatigues.

Listening to English broadcasts was forbidden and anyone caught doing so was hideously punished. Among other things of local interest we learnt of the sale of Red Cross supplies, intended for us, in the shops and on the black market at fantastic prices; of the sense of insecurity among the local population; and of the Japanese system of espionage with paid spies everywhere.

Among those who brought us reliable information about life in occupied Malaya were a number of European clergy who, owing to the sympathetic attitude of a Japanese official, Mr. Shinozaki, at the time of capitulation, were allowed to continue working in Singapore and other parts of the country until early in 1943. The Bishop of Singapore was among these. After he was interned, a Tamil priest, Dr. Chelliah of St. Andrew's School, maintained the work of the Cathedral as acting Dean of Singapore. Mrs. Cornelius, who was interned in June 1942 had had the unique experience of living in a house with her husband in the P.O.W. camp at Changi for the preceding four months, unknown to the Japanese. She was the only woman in the camp. When the Japanese commandant discovered her presence, he was much perturbed as to how to account for her disappearance from his books. She could not remain in the camp, and he had no intention of showing that she had ever been there, but her going left him one prisoner short. Somehow he must have "cooked" his books to solve the problem for there were never any enquiries about her from higher authorities.

There were a number of electrical and water engineers who were kept in the town to maintain essential services, while a few English doctors were also allowed to continue working at the different hospitals for a while. Towards the end of 1942, six men and a woman, Dr. Cicely Williams, with Mrs. de Moubray as chaperon, were taken into Singapore for several months to write a report on nutrition in Singapore. This was during the benevolent regime of Lt. Suzuki but nothing came of his good intentions. In a little speech to them the day after they left the camp, addressing them as "English gentlemen and lady", he put them on their honour not to indulge in anti-Japanese activity while outside the camp.

Nevertheless their mere presence in the town when they walked through the streets to their office, or went shopping for food was a link between us and the local inhabitants, an indication that the English had not wholly abandoned Malaya, and that there were English men and women in the country who believed that the power of Japan could not last.

The debt of the internees to the local people, especially to the Chinese, was greater than could ever be repaid. Most of the money with which we were able to buy food to supplement the inadequate rations provided by the Japanese was smuggled into the camp, at great risk, by Chinese sympathisers. The procedure as I have heard it described was as follows: When a lenient sentry was in charge of the ambulance, the Europeans got permission to have a meal at a café, the sentry joining them at their expense. On paying the bill, a signed blank cheque, prepared beforehand, was placed among the currency notes and when the receipted bill and change were handed back, concealed under them would be notes for hundreds or thousands of dollars. Sometimes presents of money were made in this way. The Chinese who freely cashed these cheques had no certainty that they would ever be met. They were gambling for our sakes on the return of the British to Malaya, and many of them paid for their courage in Kempeitai prisons with death.

Direct contact with any P.O.W. was strictly forbidden, but illicit letters passed fairly freely at one time. A cigarette tin full of letters would be flung from a supply lorry to a gang of P.O.W. working by the roadside, or the P.O.W. would throw one into the lorry. Any men caught passing these letters were punished with the utmost cruelty, our captors being in continual fear of anti-Japanese activity arising from the contacts of prisoners with each other or with the mainly hostile population. Mr. Mervyn Shepherd, a civil servant who was caught passing letter from internees to the P.O.W., was fearfully tortured because he refused to give information about other men concerned. After the water torture, he was left for dead by the Japanese but was revived by some Asian fellow prisoners.

The only official contact which ever took place between the P.O.W. and the civilian prisoners was at Christmas 1942, when Mrs. Mulvaney persuaded the Japanese general to give permission for a meeting of half an hour between relatives in the two camps. A number of men, chiefly husbands and fathers, were brought over to meet their relations outside the prison walls, but some of the women who went out came back in bitter disappointment, their menfolk having already been sent to Formosa or to Siam. Sir Shenton Thomas and other leading civilian internees and all the chief military officers had been sent to Formosa in July 1942.

From letters from home and from reports from the town, we gradually received some account of the fate of those who had left during the last few days before capitulation. We were told the names of many who had been killed when the ships were sunk, while the survivors, after various adventures on desert islands and among Malay fishing villages, had been interned in camps in Sumatra. It was a great relief to those whose relatives had safely reached Australia or India to learn that they were being well looked after by the Government or by their husbands' firms.

By interning all Europeans and many Eurasians, by deporting numbers of Eurasians and settling them in new clearings in the jungle, and by forbidding the use of English in the schools, the Japanese were trying to eradicate all traces of European influence in Malaya. In so short a time, this was impossible and was rendered still more difficult by the problem of supplying a country which, both for food and clothing as well as for all manufactured articles, was almost entirely dependent on imports. They did not attempt to work the rubber plantations and took the coolies to work on the Siam railway. It is not realised in England that besides the P.O.W. who were employed there, great numbers of Asian labourers, both Chinese and Tamils, were used. Lacking the military organisation which our men had, their sufferings were even greater, with a death-roll to match. The true numbers will never be known but according to one estimate at least 50 percent of them died. Many of the Chinese were young men of good education and good families who were kidnapped by Japanese press gangs and never seen again. Elizabeth Choy's family lost three young men in this way

The Japanese tried to form a Eurasian settlement at Bahau, Malaya. They evacuated many Eurasians and some French clergy, monks, and nuns from Singapore and other towns to Bahau. Bahau was surrounded by jungle infected with malaria and had an extremely high death rate. Those who had money could buy food, but among the poor there was intense suffering as they could not possibly become self-supporting on their jungle clearings during the few months in which food was supplied to them. Monseigneur Devals, the Roman Catholic Bishop of Malaya, died there of tetanus after an injury to his foot.

The Japanese attempted to establish agricultural colonies in various places in Malaya. They realised that Malaya had always been dependent on imported rice for the bulk of its food, and to meet a future shortage they enforced the cultivation of tapioca as a substitute on every plot of waste and open land they could find. In spite of all these efforts, it was impossible to provide for the population and for their own large armies. There was a big increase in deaths from beri-beri and other nutritional diseases. During the last few months of the Japanese occupation, the bodies of the dead were left unburied by the roadsides, even in Singapore itself.

The Japanese tried to prevent epidemics. After the return of the British, it was found that a very large medical research station had been established in Singapore. This station was stocked with all kinds of animals used in the production of serum and other medical preparations, well housed and well looked after, and was large enough to turn out sufficient supplies for the whole Far East. In camp, we were continually being vaccinated and inoculated and we never had any serious epidemics.

On 10 October 1943, the anniversary of the founding of the Chinese Republic, the Japanese started their big Kempeitai drive throughout Malaya. What led them to make this special effort we never knew, except that presumably they realised that their hold on Malaya was exceedingly precarious and they hoped that a reign of terror would strengthen it. There was also a rumour that a number of their ships had been sunk off the Malayan coast, and that they thought this was the result of information supplied by sympathetic Chinese and transmitted to British naval forces by a concealed radio in our camp. Whatever the facts about the loss of ship, our camp had nothing to do with it as we never possessed a transmitter, but they did not believe this and made many searches, and questioned and tortured many people, in an attempt to find what did not exist.

The drive was conducted by the Japanese Military Police, the Kempeitai, known among us as the Gestapo, because they had been trained on the lines of the German Gestapo and acted in the same way. For the rest of the internment, every event in camp was dated before or after "the double Tenth", by which we meant that first day of the drive. Certainly our lives before and after we came under the Kempeitai were two different kinds of existence. The atmosphere of Kempeitai rule, with its calculated brutality supreme over every consideration of humanity, justice and even common sense, is not to be conveyed in any words that I can command. Although for many years we had read about Gestapo rule in Germany, none of us had the least idea of what such a government actually means. None of the internees except a few Jewish refugees from Nazi Europe had ever before lived beneath the shadow of a universal fear, of a power devoid of pity, which apparently struck blindly without rhyme or reason in any direction to which a vague suspicion summoned it.

On the morning of 10 October, the women were all collected in the Rose Garden, nominally for roll call. Roll call had been announced unexpectedly the night before, the second since internment, and there was a feeling of something unusual in the air as we waited in alphabetical order in rows. The Japanese officials were late in coming, it was after 10 o'clock in the morning, the sun was growing hot and we were getting impatient, when suddenly there was a clatter of running feet in the entrance yard and someone shouted excitedly, "Armed soldiers!"

A moment later, Japanese officers accompanied by troops carrying rifles entered the compound and faced us. For the first time since internment, I contemplated the possibility of an immediate massacre—a thought which had occurred to everyone of us, since lined up as we were with the compound wall behind us and the troops with their rifles in front, the scene seemed ideally set. The effect no doubt had been planned deliberately to try to shake our morale. It certainly was quite impressive. The Japanese paused for a few minutes to let us appreciate the significance of the situation and then summoned Mrs. Nixon, who was then Camp Commandant, Dr. Hopkins and some others out of the ranks while the rest of us wondered if these were to be the first victims. However, it was very soon clear that we were not to be executed, not just yet anyway. The soldiers stood grinning at us with amusement rather than ferocity and presently they all went off into the prison, leaving us in the Rose Garden. After about an hour, permission was given to go into "A" compound, outside the Carpenter's Shop, where there were two lavatories and a tap. There, without food, and sheltering under what shade could be got by draping blankets over the drying lines, we spent the day. At 5 p.m., Dr. Hopkins got permission for us to go into the Carpenter's Shop and to take people who had fainted to the hospital, and at about 5.30, our visitors left.

Meanwhile, they had been searching the whole ground floor of the prison with the greatest thoroughness. The area of their search comprised the Dungeon, the Crypt, Hurricane Alley, the Infirm Ladies' Annexe and the Carpenter's Shop. In spite of their dread of infection, they also searched the hospital, the sanatorium and the convalescent verandah. The possessions of the permanent inhabitants of the ground floor were gone through by expert searchers. Photographs framed in passepartout were taken to pieces, the hems of dresses were ripped open and so on. A few books and personal papers were also removed, most of which were returned undamaged later. They paid scarcely any attention to the cells, but for some months they continued to search the ground floor at intervals with painstaking minuteness. They paid special attention to the Dungeon, the inhabitants of which were all nursing sisters. We could not understand why they concentrated so much on this room, unless it was because of the friendship of some of the sisters with the men doctors who were responsible for the activities of the ambulance, and so for communication with people in Singapore. We never knew exactly what they were looking for, but from their interest in odd bits of wire it seemed as if they were searching for a radio. They might have saved themselves all their trouble for, had they only known it, there was hardly a woman in the camp capable of putting a faulty electric light connection in order, let alone of constructing and operating a wireless set. A similar search was conducted at the men's side of the gaol.

As soon as the Kempeitai left that first evening, a panic-stricken destruction of diaries, letters from P.O.W. and all documents likely to incriminate anybody took place in both camps. Some people got it into their heads that the object of the search was to discover hoards of money or jewellery and they made frantic efforts to hide any they possessed. In a bare concrete building like the gaol, this was practically impossible, and the risk of such valuables being found and appropriated by other internees was much greater than of their being seized by the Japanese. The only money which the Kempeitai searches took was some which had been sent into the camp for us to buy food and was intended for the camp funds.

It gradually transpired that there were two motives for their interests in us: to discover and suppress our two radios, which they did; and to suppress all intercourse between the camp and the people of Malaya. They were convinced that money given to us by the Chinese had been used to foment anti-Japanese activity, and with this idea in mind they eventually took nearly sixty people out of camp, subjecting them to various kinds of imprisonment, questioning and torture. Fifteen men died from the treatment they received and one was executed. The futility of inflicting all this misery may be realised from the fact that we had no transmitter, as they feared, and no amount of torture or questioning could reveal one. The money given us by the

Chinese had not been used in anti-enemy activity but merely to keep ourselves alive.

We learned later that in carrying out much of this investigation, the Japanese had been acting on false information supplied by one of our own men, incriminating a number of his fellow-internees. What led him to do such a thing we never knew, but when the Japanese realised that he had deceived them, they shot him.

Three women were taken out of the camp. The first was Mrs. Bloom, the wife of an English P.O.W. doctor. Before her marriage, she had done a little journalism in Singapore, and apparently on this account only, the Japanese kept her in prison for five months. During the whole period, she was only twice questioned, and nothing was ever proven or even alleged against her. A few days after they had taken Mrs. Bloom, Dr. Cicely Williams was sent for. She was more closely questioned on account of her contact with the local people while working in Singapore during the previous year, but she too was never charged with anything definite and spent five months in Kempeitai prisons.

These prisons were constructed on the same general plan, existing buildings being adapted for the purpose. The former Y.M.C.A. premises at Orchard Road became such a prison. The cells, which varied in size, had one side made of stout wooden bars so that the prisoners could be under continual observation. There was a small barred window high up in the wall and a lavatory in a corner. Otherwise the cell was bare. Europeans and Asians were herded in indiscriminately in the cells without any possibility of privacy. Sometimes the cells were so crowded that there was no room for everyone to lie down at night and they had to sleep by turns. For fourteen hours every day, from 8 a.m. to 10 p.m., they had to sit cross-legged except for ten minutes' exercise after meals.

By day, the cells were dim, but at night they were lit by glaring bulbs and it was forbidden to cover the eyes. The prisoners were given no bedding or soap, but a little toilet paper was occasionally provided. The water of the lavatory had to be used for a variety of purposes and they had nothing with which to clean the lavatory or the cell. Soon the prisoners became sick with dysentery and other diseases, but no medical help was given. The prisoners were supposed to be supervised continuously by Japanese sentries who enforced the various rules, but sometimes the guards were slack and then they could relax a little.

In the course of questioning, many men were tortured, some of them many times, and were returned to the cell in a dreadful condition. No medical attention was given, nor were their companions supposed to speak to them or help them. Little therefore could be done for them, but I was told that an internee who was badly beaten owed the use of his legs to the massage and other care given by Dr. Williams when the sentries were not watching.

Occasionally the Kempeitai provided a treat by giving three chunks of pineapple or some biscuits to the women. One Christmas Eve, the prisoners in one cell asked the sentry to call them at midnight as they wanted to say their prayers, but he did not come till 2 a.m. To their surprise, he then said that he had thought they wanted to be called at the local time, not Tokyo time.

One of those who suffered most severely was the Bishop of Singapore. The Japanese wanted him to account for a sum of $10,000 which they knew had been sent into camp for him by Chinese sympathisers as a present. The money has been misappropriated. He knew nothing of it and therefore could not account for it. Obsessed with the idea that the internees were fomenting anti-Japanese activity with the money, the Kempeitai took it for granted that this present had been used for such a purpose. They nearly killed both the Bishop and the camp treasurer before they found out what had happened. Both of them were still very ill when at last returned to camp, but eventually both recovered.

As far as the rest of us were concerned, the Kempeitai prisoners simply disappeared out of sight and knowledge. Questions about them were not answered or were put off with lies. We were not allowed to send them anything though they had not been permitted to take even a change of clothes with them.

Early in January, some men prisoners were returned to camp. They were ill and bore the marks of torture but they were strictly forbidden to talk about their imprisonment or the interrogations. Our next news was the deaths of some men in Miyako Hospital. Among them was Mr. Adrian Clarke, for a long time Men's Commandant, a brilliant man and outstanding in camp for his personal integrity and fine character.

The two women prisoners were unexpectedly returned to us in March 1944. Dr. Williams could walk. Mrs. Bloom was a stretcher case. They were emaciated, with discoloured dead-looking skins from being shut up for so long and were suffering from beri-beri, skin trouble and sores. They were put into hospital for some weeks before they were fit to return to normal camp life. After a further period of rest and recuperation, they were eventually able to carry on with their former activities, though they were always liable to spells of sickness and to the return of septic sores and other results of prolonged malnutrition. Nearly all the Kempeitai prisoners who did not actually die of neglect and torture made a fairly satisfactory recovery after returning to the camp, considering the conditions under which they had to live and the lack of adequate food and facilities for treatment. Such ghastly experiences have a psychological as well as a physical effect, and neither could be expected to disappear quickly, particularly when proper food and freedom from the strain of prison life were out of the question.

The two returned prisoners received the most heartfelt welcome from the women's camp. The few extras available for hospital patients were given them as freely as possible, supplemented by presents of tinned food from private hoards. Among these was a present of a tin of butter, unprocurable at that time, from a recent German internee. There was one unpleasant episode, arising out of the detestable feuds of camp politics. It affected Mrs. Bloom. She had never been *persona grata* with the women who were then running the camp, and they considered that this was a good opportunity to gratify their dislike. Only two days before she returned, the Committee had decided that her "space" on Hurricane Alley could not be left unoccupied any longer. It had been given to another internee, on the strict promise that other arrangements would be made for her if and when Mrs. Bloom returned. Mrs. Bloom came back to the camp and after some weeks was ready to be discharged from hospital, where her bed was needed for another patient, but her "space" was still occupied and she had nowhere to go.

To every woman, even in the best of health, the secure possession of that small spot in the gaol which could be considered as "home" was of overwhelming importance, and much more so to someone weakened in health and spirit by the horrors of a Kempeitai prison. Representations were made to the Committee but with no effect. They refused to make the necessary arrangements. During this period, Mrs. Bloom might be seen slowly wandering across the compound with dragging steps, carrying her stool and other possessions, sick, dazed and wretched, to sit where she could, having no spot in our crowded gaol to call her own. After another two weeks, in which it became apparent that her health was suffering from the long delay in returning to normal camp life, and as the Committee continued to do nothing, Dr. Cicely Williams went to them and threatened to go on hunger strike unless proper arrangements were made. Space for the other internee was found the same evening and the next morning Mrs. Bloom returned to her place.

The third woman to suffer at the hands of the Kempeitai was Mrs. Nixon. She was taken out after the return of the other two and charged with a definite offence, namely the distribution of the typewritten sheets of wireless news. After a few weeks in the cells under dreadful conditions, she was condemned to six months' imprisonment. She was transferred to a civil prison where she was better treated. Most of the time she had a cell to herself or with one or two women prisoners only. The Japanese in charge gave her tinned milk twice a day and some cushions to sleep on. Once when she had fever, the commanding officer stay up with her all night putting cold compresses on her forehead. Notwithstanding this relatively humane regime, she came back to camp in Sime Road as a stretcher case, and was many weeks in hospital before she was fit to lead the normal camp life again.

None of the English women were actually tortured but many Asians were. Elizabeth Choy, who spent two different periods in the hands of the Kempeitai, was made to live in one of the prison passages where people passed day and night. She was also made to carry a chair from the bottom of the building to the top and down again for many days. When exhausted by this she was ordered to carry a heavy table instead. Her husband was a Kempeitai prisoner for two years, and was only released after the return of the English to Singapore. Like the other local people, they suffered because of the help they gave the internees and for their friendliness to us.

Within the camp, the Kempeitai withdrew all amenities such as relatives' meetings, inter-camp post, lectures and church services. All rules were enforced with the utmost strictness, especially the rule relating to no communication between the two camps. The men were not allowed to enter our camp at all, except very occasionally to do plumbing or electrical repairs. They were no longer allowed to bring our food, and as we could not carry the heavy tubs up and down the steps to the Carpenter's Shop, we had to queue for it in one long line in the passage leading to the central courtyard. In a thousand petty ways, our lives were deliberately oppressed and made burdensome. Meeting in groups of more than four was forbidden so that all entertainment and most classes were impossible. By scattering the art class in different corners of the compound and running all the morning from one pupil to another, Mrs. Bateman managed to keep it going for some time, though at the expense of her health.

The school was closed. The number of children was nearly doubled by an influx of new interns in December and January. The problem of these unoccupied children running wild in the prison became very serious. It was finally solved by volunteers who spent the day conducting games for them in the Rose Garden and telling them stories. There were many cases of dysentery and whooping cough. The hospital could not accommodate all the cases, and even the Japanese taking roll call, held regularly every week, seemed perturbed at the number of women who were lying sick in the cells. The food was drastically cut down both in quantity and quality. Private cooking was forbidden.

Japanese sentries, both ordinary soldiers and military police, were continually in and out of the camp, searching people's property, or merely looking around. They often made their rounds after lights out, tramping up and down noisily to frighten us, and waking everyone two or three times in the night. There was no question of keeping them out of the camp. Sometimes they came creeping round in rubber shoes and carrying torches which they flashed on us in our beds without warning. Many people became very frightened and some began to have screaming nightmares as on the first days of internment. A sense of utter insecurity reigned, made still more acute by our ignorance and apprehension as to the fate of the men and women in the hands of the Kempeitai and the ever present dread of more being taken out to join them. Every now and then, more men were taken out, a sick and injured prisoner was returned, or we received news of the death of another. All of these, combined with the incessant din which followed the new internees' arrival, began to tell very severely on everyone's health and nerves.

In addition, we were for many months confined entirely to the gaol, and our exercise space in the compounds was much reduced by the building of two large thatched huts intended for more internees. By April, after nearly seven months of Kempeitai rule, the camp as a whole was near breaking point. Fortunately for us, the Japanese decided that they wanted the gaol for P.O.W., so we had to be transferred to another camp. People who were seriously ill, and those who suffered nervous breakdowns, pulled through well enough, thanks to the move to Sime Road.

Changi, February 1944

The gates, they are not shut, but only guarded:
The windows are not sealed, but closely barred:
The walls, they are not spiked, only unscaleable:
The stars are not shut out, only the landscape.

The torrent of human voices is like a torment,
It is like a mill, grinding hearing to nothing,
It is like a sea, pounding a wrecked man to pieces,
It is like a hammer, crushing a stick on an anvil.

10 Sime Road

One day in May 1944, a Japanese official told us that we would shortly be given some very good news. We still thought only of repatriation, and the deepest depression followed when told that we were merely being moved to Sime Road. This had formerly been a British military camp. It was on the outskirts of the city, near the MacRitchie Reservoir and close to a golf course. We received the most contradictory accounts of this place.

According to some women who were taken to look at it in order to allot accommodation, it consisted of old, filthy, dilapidated army huts, had scarcely any sanitation, no building suitable for a hospital, and was altogether a change for the worse. The men were much more optimistic and could not understand "what you women are making such a fuss about". The stimulus of a change of scene and routine, the chance of an outdoor life with plenty of fresh air and open space and, above all, freedom from the walls which for more than two years had been our horizon, worked what seemed like miracles.

The Japanese could not understand our depression at leaving the gaol. It was partly due to a dread of all the effort that would be needed to make our new camp habitable, and partly to the fear that our baggage would be limited. This meant leaving behind the indispensable equipment which had been so laboriously collected, and starting all over again. The camp grew more cheerful when General Saito, then in charge of all the enemy aliens in Malaya, told us that all our property was to go with us in lorries provided by the Japanese army. He was as good as his word. The lorries, with Japanese drivers, went to and fro between the gaol and the new camp until every piece of luggage had been delivered. The able-bodied internees also went in lorries, and ambulances were provided for the sick and infirm. It amused us to see the ambulance drivers with gauze masks tied carefully over their mouths and noses for fear they should pick up some infection from the patients inside.

The new camp was surrounded with barbed wire outside which were flimsy thatched hurdles called *kajang*, six feet high, which were supposed to prevent the passers-by from looking in and us from looking out. Within the *kajang* was a large area of bare open ground, with only a few clumps of trees, and scattered with small wild rhododendron bushes and aromatic shrubs. The Japanese had been using it as a transit camp for P.O.W. sent to Thailand or Japan. As none had ever stayed long enough to do much work on it, it was in a neglected state. There were a few areas in which vegetables had been cultivated and which now abounded in weeds. Most of the ground was overgrown with lallang, a tall tough, wild grass with a keen edge that cuts like a knife. The men's and women's camps were separated only by a barbed wire fence and a sentry at the gate. A good road, somewhat out of repair, ran right through the camp.

On the highest point of the undulating ground about which our huts were dotted, stood the Japanese office. It was formerly the house of a man internee, and was known to us as the Green House. In the women's camp area were the graves of two British soldiers of

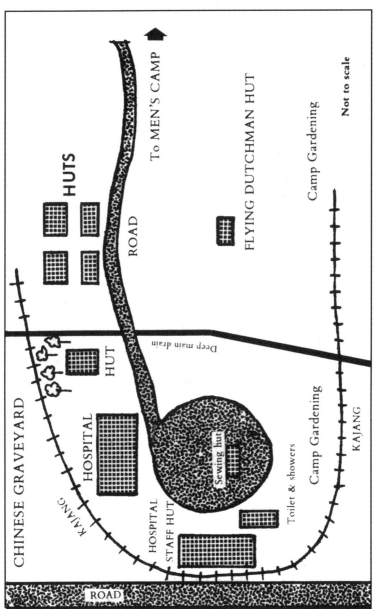

Plan of Women's Camp at Sime Road.

the Cambridge Regiment. In the men's camp was a small cemetery of soldiers' graves, and on the cross surmounting one of them, a woman internee found her husband's name. It was her first intimation of his death.

The women's camp was on the sides of two small hills, with a little valley in which we cultivated vegetables. A six-foot deep concrete drain ran down the middle. The road ran across the valley, from the camp entrance at the foot of what we called the Hospital Hill, round the lower slope of the other hill, and into the men's camp. Beyond the road was a sunken area where sweet potatoes, bananas, papayas and other plants were grown for food. There was also a small grove of tall, dark rambutan trees beneath which the youngest children had school, and the Church of England services were generally held.

The first thing to be done was to allot accommodation, clean up the huts and establish the hospital, the camp office and the dispensary. The office was placed in one corner of a dilapidated, three-sided shack called The Flying Dutchman. It had been the officers' bar and the walls were decorated with lively cartoons by Ronald Searle, who had been a P.O.W. there. The dispensary was housed in another corner of this shack, with half a dozen women living in cubicles behind the counter. The Japanese had wanted to use this hut as living quarters for about forty people, but it was so leaky that they agreed to turn the Sikh police out of a hut near the camp entrance and transfer the women there instead.

The "hospital" hut was devoid of all conveniences whatever and did not even possess a lavatory until the men built two. Other necessary additions were made in the course of time but it always remained very cramped and inconvenient, though it was luxurious by comparison with hospitals in most of the P.O.W. camps, where many patients had no bedding of any sort. Most of the huts held about sixty people. They were built of wood roofed with attap (palm-thatch), on concrete foundations with asbestos ceilings, and the majority were divided into small rooms by asbestos sheet partitions. Walls and roofs were punctured with holes made by shell and bomb fragments during the fighting before capitulation, which had been severe in this neighbourhood. Living space was apportioned at about twenty-four square feet per woman. Even at this rate, it was impossible to get everyone into the huts, and eventually rain-swept verandahs and covered passages had to be made habitable with chicks, sacking, and sheets of asbestos.

Before we left the gaol, we had scribbled messages for the incoming P.O.W. on the cell walls. On the walls of the Sime Road huts were the messages which they had left for us. These gave us a terrible shock because it was the first news we had had of the P.O.W. sent to work in Thailand. We found notices like the following: "B force went up 2,000 strong, returned 600."

Another gave a death-roll and concluded, "Causes of death—Typhus, dysentery, malaria, ulcers, beri-beri, starvation."

There were messages about the living, one of which gave me news of my brother, as well as lists of the dead. These notices filled us with horror. We had always imagined that the men in Thailand were better off than the rest. Scores of people had relatives and friends among the Thailand P.O.W. of whom they could not obtain any up-to-date news, and the information given by these ghastly notices increased their anxiety a hundredfold. In most cases, no reliable news was received until some time after liberation. A list of the dead was compiled from the names of the hut walls in the two camps, and circulated with great secrecy because we were not supposed to communicate in any way with the P.O.W., and the soldiers might have been punished for leaving messages.

The Eurasian wife of a P.O.W. heard about the list and went to the Flying Dutchman to make enquiries about it. She asked Dr. Robinson about it. The doctor, who had not got it, and knew the woman to be anti-British and unbalanced as well, did not want to discuss it with her and said she knew nothing about it. The woman flew into a rage and pulling off her wooden shoe began to hit the doctor with it. The doctor got it away from her and threw it on the road. The woman then pulled off her other shoe and again attacked the doctor who again, without striking her assailant, managed to get it way from her.

By this time, the woman was beside herself with fury. She ran up the hill to the Green House to complain to Mr. Tominaga that she had been attacked and beaten by a European. Dr. Robinson meanwhile went off on a routine inspection of the camp drains, taking with her a long stick which she used for the purpose. Very soon after this she was ordered to go to Mr. Tominaga's office, where the woman who had reported her was waiting. Tominago apparently did not consider it necessary to ask any questions. He sprang to his feet, snatched away her stick and began to beat her with it, bruising her badly. The woman watched with a complacent grin. This outburst seemed to assuage his wrath for nothing was ever heard about the list.

Feeling among the Europeans ran very high against the woman informer. Some had wanted to go that night and beat her up. Among some of the Eurasian and Asian internees, there was perceptible a certain feeling of amusement and even of satisfaction at this open humiliation of a European, but others were sympathetically shocked. All were alarmed because they knew the same thing might happen to them.

Some weeks later, Dr. Robinson attended to a patient who shared a room with the informer. Apparently she still thought she could get away with anything, and flung a basin of water over the doctor, but for this she afterwards apologised. She was an odd person of such insane temper that sometimes she was hardly responsible for what she did. She often beat her three unfortunate children, yet when the youngest child was very ill with a whooping cough, she nursed it day and night with great devotion.

A troublesome element in the camp came to the fore at Sime Road. The Japanese went in and out of the women's quarters freely and some of them found girlfriends among the younger Eurasians. We nicknamed these the "Japanese Comfort Girls". These girls shared the crowded huts on the same terms as the rest of the internees, and the Japanese visited them there, by day or night, without any regard for the other inhabitants. Later, the different couples built themselves little shacks, or "bowers" as they were called, covered with sacking, *kajang*, or creepers and received their boyfriends there instead. A small cottage called the White House was built under Japanese orders for some of the Comfort Girls. A middle-aged Englishwoman who was the wife of a Chinese and two or three ex-prostitutes lived there.

The Japanese used no compulsion on these women. The chance of obtaining extra food made any other inducement unnecessary. Some of the sentries who found Comfort Girls in the camp were well-behaved, decent men, but most of them were continually drunk, noisy and quarrelsome. On one occasion, one tried to stab his girl after an evening party, but was fortunately too drunk to succeed. In addition to the unpleasantness of the fights, feasts and other uproar which disturbed the sleep of those in the neighbourhood, there was the uncomfortable certainty that everything which happened in camp was reported by them to the Japanese. Our officials did not dare to impose camp discipline on these women. Their neighbours had to put up with all sorts of arrogance, insolence and misbehaviour without complaint, for fear of being informed on.

Mr. Tominaga paid very little attention to the camp, though he sometimes wandered round the men's area and inspected the parcel post to help himself to a book. The general running of the camp was

Hut at Sime Road Camp. Inset shows a picture of Mary Thomas in 1946.

in the hands of Kobiyashi who hated all Europeans and made no attempts to disguise it. He was vindictive and spiteful and was always trying to create trouble. He did not look very Japanese and was said to have European and Korean blood. Also exercising some general administrative authority was Kawazai, nicknamed by us as Blue-Stockings and by the men as Puss-in-Boots. He did not seem to be quite right in the head. Without being particularly hostile to Europeans, he was dangerously bad-tempered and would often knock the men about. The smallest drop of drink made him quite beside himself.

At Changi, he was prowling round the women's camp at about half past ten one night when he came across a nursing sister, Sue Williams, who was preparing to go to sleep. Once in bed we were never expected to get out and bow to any Japanese, but Blue-Stockings was drunk. He flew into a rage because she did not bow to him and rushed to beat her with the stick which he always carried. She slipped out on the other side just in time and ran off into the darkness, but Blue-Stockings continued to beat the bed clothes for some time.

Some of the Japanese were good-natured. Yamamoto was a civil, quiet, respectable person, always neatly dressed and wearing white gloves. He did his best to control Nagara, a rough, drunken oak who was always creating disturbances and hitting people.

A stout, kind, rather dull-witted person, nicknamed Dopey, took a great fancy to a three-year-old English girl. She was the daughter of a P.O.W. and had been born in the camp. He gave her eggs and carried her about on his shoulder. Mary Bell reciprocated his friendly feelings and used to run up to the Green House to look for him. Unfortunately someone explained to Dopey the association of his name and he was deeply hurt. He ceased to play with the children.

Another amiable sentry was a cheery fellow called Joe. He was never unpleasant and in fact made a point of taking a friendly, fatherly interest in his charges. I was painting one day, when Joe walked past with his rifle. He stopped to cheer me up. "Ah, *banyak chantek! Banyak chantek!*" (Very pretty! Very pretty!) he said with enthusiasm and beamed benevolently at me and my drawing, an unrecognisable sketch of rambutan trees done in Chinese ink.

One tiresome and disagreeable sentry was nicknamed Acid-Drop. He was not particularly brutal or unjust, but he was extremely pernickety in enforcing all the irksome petty rules and restrictions relating to such things as bowing, smoking, and our behaviour at roll-call. He always seemed to be on the watch to catch somebody out, especially the Europeans. It was his job to supervise and take roll-call which had been discontinued when we moved to Sime Road, until the last few months, during which it took place daily. It is hard to say who suffered most, we from having to get up in the dark, wait about for him when he was late, and then put up with the annoyance of bowing to him when he came, or he from the incurably ragged bow and the unseemly disrespectful whispers which it was his daily penance to endure.

He took his duties very seriously indeed. In a desperate effort to improve our performance, he summoned a meeting of the floor-walkers, and appealed earnestly to them to cooperate in raising the standard of our bow and make us a credit to the camp. After this we were rather more careful as we knew the floor-walkers were liable to punishment if he became really annoyed. He was so pleased with the improvement that a fortnight later he gave them a quarter pound of sugar each.

The Japanese wandered about the camp freely on official sentry duty or visits to their friends. When someone suddenly called out, "Japanese coming!" there was an immediate outcry of "Who? Who?" If the answer was "It's only Dopey," or "It's only Joe," we all settled down quietly again. If the reply was "Blue-Stockings," or "Acid-Drop," everyone jumped hurriedly to attention or retired out of sight until they had gone past.

A few weeks after our arrival at Sime Road, a camp inspection by a "very important general" was announced. The men were then kept busy for days clearing up rubbish, cutting grass, and trimming the edges of the roads to make everything fit for him. There were two schools of thought on the subject of inspections. Some women held that defiance of circumstances and an unbreakable morale were best expressed by putting on plenty of make-up and any clean and tidy clothes one still possessed. The other school were not going to dress up for any Japanese, and held that one ought to wear one's oldest rags and any possible bandages, to make it impossible for them to pretend we were being properly looked after.

On this great occasion, we were strictly commanded to tidy all huts and verandahs and to put the hospital into particularly trim order. Special preparations were made in front of the hospital where a men's fatigue had to put up an awning. It blew down twice and at last the Japanese undertook the job themselves. Those who lived in the hospital staff hut nearby spent an agreeable two hours watching them struggle with sacking, tarpaulin, poles and bits of rope. They got it up in the end. A table was "borrowed" from the sewing-room and some chairs from the hospital which, after several trial arrangements, were satisfactorily disposed on the asphalt below the awning, and everything was ready. The next afternoon, some nursing sisters, a doctor or two, some V.A.Ds., and the hospital cleaners including myself were drawn up in the sun outside, ready to bow when the great men appeared. The whole camp had a special lesson in bowing for the occasion.

The hospital staff on duty had been increased for the afternoon. They were looking most impressive in clean, white uniforms complete with veils. Dr. Hopkins had on a new blouse and freshly creased trousers, and the matron was extremely spruce in dark navy. The scene received its first setback with the arrival of Dr. Elliot, absent-minded and cheerful, in her usual rags, and a few minutes later Dr. Williams appeared, clop-clopping in wooden sandals, dressed in a faded jacket and old blue trousers with a heart-shaped black patch on the seat. These two seemed unaware of the solemnity of the occasion. They sat down on the edge of the hospital verandah beside the open drain and began an animated chat.

At last, the general appeared, walking slowly past the bowing internees who were drawn up outside their huts. Finally he breasted our hill and, rounding the corner of the sewing-room, appeared before us. At the word of command, we stood to attention and bowed, but he was not looking. Very proudly the officers escorted him to the somewhat lopsided awning. Proudly they seated him on a chair, and withdrawing to a respectful distance, stood gazing at him with deep admiration. We waited expectantly for him to make a speech or to give us some Red Cross parcels, or at least to inspect the hospital, but nothing happened.

It was a hot day. The general was fat, and had walked round the whole of the two camps. We waited for one of his attendants to bring him a glass of lemonade but still nothing happened. The general began to look bored and slightly self-conscious. At the end of seventy seconds, he rose to his feet, and turning on his heel with an air of determination, he marched off down the hill with his escort in respectful pursuit. The great inspection was over.

The whole atmosphere of the camp was very much changed by our new surroundings. We had a fairly wide expanse of open land round us, with views in various directions. There was a Chinese market garden beyond the wire at the bottom of the camp. We could see the family working away among their crops. Cattle grazed in a Chinese graveyard on a hill nearby, where Japanese troops, uttering strange war cries, used to have battle practice, their heads camouflaged with festoons of leaves and grass. Sometimes there was a Chinese funeral with a loud shrilling of pipes and beating of drums. The road ran quite close to the *kajang*. Through cracks in the fence, one could see the passers-by, coolies, troops, Japanese grooms exercising polo ponies, and gangs of men internees, barefooted and naked except for loin-cloths, pulling loads of firewood with the Japanese sentry riding on top of the cart. The troops sang Japanese songs to rather simple, European-sounding tunes, and seemed to make a point of bursting into song as they drew level with the camp. Like the Lady of Shalott, we watched the world go by but took no part in it.

At night, we sat about in groups in the moonlight, speculating on the latest war news and rumours, calculating the chances of victory and repatriation, exchanging the newest piece of gossip about the Comfort Girls and their friends, and telling one another about our lives and activities before we were interned, or discussing the books we were reading.

Each day, people went out to watch the sunrise and sunset, enjoying the astonishing blaze of colours, which was sometimes so brilliantly reflected in the opposite corner of the sky that one did not know whether to look east or west.

There was one disadvantage in our new camp when compared with the gaol. Although there was far more space around us, there was hardly any privacy. Except for a few who were tucked away on verandahs or in odd corners, no one could ever enjoy the least personal privacy by day or night. In Changi, one could often shut oneself into the cell for an hour or two's peace and solitude and many people, whose cellmates preferred to sleep in the compounds, had their cells to themselves at night.

For sixteen months at Sime Road, we did not known what privacy or quietness was. Whether it was a small room with only eight inhabitants or a larger one with over thirty, the atmosphere was the same. In the unwilling intimacy of this life, it would not have been surprising if people's tempers had given way much more than they actually did. The self-control of most women was remarkable and nervous outbursts were few. This was partly because we all knew that however fed-up we might be feeling ourselves, all the others were no happier, and partly because such useless explosions were far too exhausting to be indulged in. As the food shortage grew worse, we became first more nervy and then more and more apathetic.

When we reached Sime Road, we were for some time given plenty of rice but otherwise the quality of the food continued to be bad. We had finished our stocks of tinned meat and fish some months before, except for a small reserve which was kept for the hospitals. The supply of vegetables was also limited. Our only protein was from *blachan* which was supplied in small quantities from time to time. The diet was very deficient in protein, fat, calcium and various vitamins. Large and increasing cuts in the rice ration from February 1945 onwards were followed by a big increase in malnutrition cases, especially among the men who were doing heavier work than we were. These conditions included beri-beri, pellagra, tropical ulcers, and obstinate septic cuts, abrasions and sores. While there was plenty of rice, people sometimes dried their surplus ration in the sun and stored it in tins to be re-cooked when the lean time, which we all knew must be ahead somewhere, should come. Rice kept like this was perfectly usable though it had a stale taste.

The Japanese knew that a food shortage was inevitable and they ordered us to grow as much food as possible in the camp. The number working on gardening fatigues was increased and large areas of lallang-covered waste were brought under cultivation. Fatigues were also sent to cultivate the ground outside the camp. The chief crops were sweet potatoes and *ubi kayu* (tapioca), but other vegetables such as chillies, spinach, lady's fingers and all sorts of beans were grown as well. Our soup was made mainly of sweet potato leaves, which were also boiled and used as a substitute for spinach. We were short of salt and the food had little flavour.

Many people supplemented their rations by growing vegetables on small patches of wasteland which they dug up and made into little private gardens. The benefit derived from these was chiefly in the form of salads, unofficial cooking fires being forbidden. Those who worked in the hospital were greatly privileged in being allowed to use one of the two dilapidated cookers there. The sisters on night duty would often help the unprivileged by cooking a "cake" of sweet potato or a vegetable curry. The Japanese more or less winked at the private fires which were made by the Eurasians and Asians, but the majority of the Europeans had no cooking facilities at all and could not even boil water to make a cup of tea. Our rations were still prepared in the men's kitchens, the primitive cooking arrangements being such that it was considered too hard and exhausting work for women.

The food was distributed in large wooden tubs which were carried round to different huts by a men's fatigue. We queued for it outside the huts; in the rain if the weather was stormy. We had no camp dining-room nor any covered place for any communal activity but thanks to the tropical climate we could do most things out of doors. The glare made it out of the question to sit out of doors during most of the day. It was impossible to find anywhere to read in peace since there were always at least half a dozen different conversations going on within earshot. As time went on, we found that our memories and powers of concentration were a good deal impaired. It was difficult to fix one's attention on anything for long, even on a conversation with a friend, and our memories of quite familiar things grew very unreliable. No doubt this was due partly to malnutrition, but also to the strain of constantly bottling up our reactions, and to the usual prisoners' sense of frustration and disgust with life, which made us try to distract our attention from our surroundings and to inhibit our responses to them. We did not worry very much about these symptoms, assuming that they were something which would disappear with our return to freedom and normal life.

During this time, I re-read *Gaudy Night*, Dorothy Sayer's detective novel about Oxford. I am not an academically-minded person, but the atmosphere of this book made me so homesick for civilisation and a humane way of life that I decided that if I got home I would take my Master's degree.

Most of our former privileges had been restored after we reached Sime Road. We had the relatives' meetings, camp post, concerts and services, but in spite of this and of the great benefits which we received from our new surroundings, the atmosphere of the camp was not what it had been before the Double Tenth. There had been a certain element of carelessness and vigour and of unconscious optimism which was gone. This change was the result of the Kempeitai regime which had brought us into contact with a system of oppression such as we had never imagined before. Its shadow had lain over every moment of life for the whole seven months in Changi after the Double Tenth.

There were still a number of internees in the Kempeitai's hands. Every now and again, a few were returned to camp: some recovered slowly, some died within a few days or hours of their arrival. The power of the Kempeitai was close behind the clumsy coolies who were immediately in charge of our lives: it still ruled in Singapore, and we now knew exactly what that implied. In addition, the Japanese in charge of us were much more freely and frequently about in the camp than before the Double Tenth. They were always around, superintending fatigues, visiting their friends, both Comfort Girls and otherwise, having evening supper with them in the huts, stealing our vegetables, escorting doctors and patients, or walking round on sentry duty.

Occasionally, they made themselves deliberately unpleasant as on Easter Monday morning when, out of spite, they sent a men's fatigue to dig up all our private gardens behind the hospital staff hut. The loss of our gardens was more than the loss of material thing. They had cost us much hard work. Very hungry as we all were, we looked forward to the small extras which we could coax the unfruitful soil to produce. They enabled us to give presents to friends. They were one of our few pleasant activities in life. Some of the Japanese stole extensively from both the private and camp gardens, sometimes taking the fruit and vegetables in person, sometimes dining off curries of stolen produce which their girlfriends had collected for them.

Blue-Stockings was one day walking down a path bordered with chilli bushes and inspecting them in vain for chillies to pick. Seeing Mrs. "Stiffey" White on the hut verandah, he asked her in a severe tone why the bushes had no chillies on them.

"They have been stolen," answered Mrs. White blandly. "When the bushes grow so near the path, people are always stealing from them. You can make the internees work extra hard, but you cannot make the chilli bushes do extra work." Blue-Stockings went off looking rather foolish.

The Japanese grew very perturbed about the stealing from the camp gardens which increased as hunger increased. There was a sort of little black market in stolen fruits and vegetables. The men gardeners would help themselves during the afternoon siesta, when most people were indoors because of the heat, and leave their pickings in hiding places for their women friends to find in return for cash of tobacco. The Japanese once caught some Asian women thieves and punished them with a beating and made them kneel in the sun for hours. Men offenders were punished by a fine, by a few days in the camp cells and by being taken off the gardening fatigue. The men's camp had a public prosecutor and a bench of magistrates to enforce discipline, while the women, for the last few months only, had a panel of about seventeen people from whom five at a time were chosen to hear and try cases of infringement of camp rules.

Punishments consisted of loss of privileges, that is, of the opportunity to buy extra sugar and of camp issues of tobacco and cigarettes, of sending letter and parcels by the camp post and of attending relatives' meetings. The last was the only punishment which anybody minded as all the others could be circumvented in one way or another, but it was of little use because, whatever the offence might be, there were always sympathisers to beg the offender off and engineer protests on her behalf. In practice, there was no effective discipline of any kind in the women's camp except that of public opinion, which was usually in favour of doing nothing.

The burden of any misbehaviour in the camp was usually borne by the camp officials, who got all the blame from the Japanese when anything went wrong although they had no real power to prevent it. The Japanese were always reluctant to enforce an order or to punish an offender themselves, preferring to take it out on the committee.

In Sime Road, the secret wireless service came into operation again but with much greater precaution than before. The genuine news was mingled with all sorts of fantastic rumours which were promulgated along with it so as to mislead the Japanese. Thus in June 1945 the camp was distressed to hear of the death of Princess Margaret after an operation for mastoid. The men still had access to the local papers, mostly printed in Chinese or Malay, which were smuggled into camp by the Sikh guards at $100 per copy.

Of course the news was Japanese in origin and often misleading and contradictory. The Japanese had a habit of refraining from publishing items of news until they were several months old. They also dated them later than the events which had succeeded them, so that every item had to be carefully scrutinised and could only be accepted with reservations. In a confused way, we knew of the fighting in Germany, and we received the news of its collapse.

There was an amusing story of the Japanese Commandant of Changi P.O.W. camp in connection with this. He knew that the men in his camp had secret radios but he made no objection provided that the listening sessions were conducted with discretion, so that he would not get into trouble with his superiors. After the fall of Germany, he sent for the British Commanding Officer and asked him if he had heard of it. The C.O. replied cautiously that he had no information about anything.

"Well," replied the Commandant, "if you don't know about it you're the only bloody fool in camp who doesn't!"

The greatest thrill of our internment occurred on Guy Fawkes Day, 1944, when a huge raid took place on the Naval Base and the Docks. According to rumours later, the Japanese had had a large concentration of shipping in Singapore waters at that time and the raid was to put it out of action. Wild with excitement and caring nothing for possible bomb or shell fragments, we stood outside the huts watching the waves of planes sail across the sky—more English planes than we had ever seen before in Malaya. The Japanese had scarcely an aeroplane to send up against them. Ineffectual puffs of white smoke from their anti-aircraft guns dotted the sky. It was in exact contrast to the raids we had experienced before the fall of Singapore. We soon saw where the different batteries were placed and held our breath until each successive wave of aircraft in turn had passed safely through the danger zone. Afterwards we heard that one or two had been brought down but we could not be sure if this was true. We could have wept for joy at the sight of the English planes and at the thought of our own people above us and so near. Their presence seemed to be a sign of the victory we never doubted must ultimately come. Later, we had the satisfaction of seeing black smoke from fires at the Naval Base rising on the horizon.

Although we were prisoners, some of us never lost the feeling that we were, in some sense, combatants too. We knew we were a nuisance and an embarrassment to the Japanese military, who would gladly have shot all prisoners. Our presence made it much more difficult for them to impose themselves on the people of Malaya. Much as they would have liked to say: "Look, the English overlords have all run away and left you!", it was impossible for them to do so. It was even impossible for them to say that we had sent all our own women and children to safety, leaving the Asians to bear the brunt of defeat alone. In this way, we felt we were fighting the influence of the Japanese. In sharing the trials and troubles of enemy occupation with the local-born people of Malaya, we felt we were forging with them a link of friendship which could not be broken, since there is no bond closer than that of shared danger and oppression. The Japanese Occupation left in Malaya an opportunity of understanding between East and West such as has never been known before. We were so self-sacrificingly helped by the local people during the internment and so warmly welcomed by them afterwards.

Our contacts with Singapore town still continued in a modified form. Occasionally, men still went out on supply lorries and the priests conducted the camp funerals which friends and relatives of the dead, though not from the women's camp, were allowed to attend. A camp scandal arose in connection with the funerals. If the sentry was agreeable, it was possible to do some shopping. There was much competition for seats in the lorry among would-be shoppers. Funerals began to resemble holiday outings without any respect for the dead.

At a funeral conducted by one of the Roman Catholic clergy, the behaviour of some of the passengers was so bad that he refused to allow anybody to attend the funerals which he conducted. Soon afterwards, the Japanese allowed only the officiating clergy to attend. They themselves always showed respect to the dead. When a man of importance died, as in the case of Archdeacon Graham White's funeral, one of the officers came into the chapel in full uniform at the beginning of the service, and saluted the coffin.

There was a particular sentry who always accompanied the lorry to the cemetery. He was tiny, aged, bow-legged man whom the men called the Jockey, and we called Grandfather. He was quite a popular person, kindly and indulgent, and weighed down with a burden of perpetual sorrow, due to a conviction that England was bound to win.

Though the women were not allowed to go to the cemetery, they could attend the funeral service. The services were always held in the men's camp where there was a small chapel build by the P.O.W. The bodies of the dead women were carried from our mortuary by men bearers, the priest in his surplice leading, the women mourners with their wreaths and bunches of flowers following behind. It was about a mile from our hospital to the chapel. Once or twice when there were two coffins to go at one time, the Japanese allowed a lorry to be used for transport. Once, there was a great shortage of wood and we could not afford a coffin for everyone who died. There was one coffin with a removable bottom which was used over and over again. After it was lowered into the grave the top was detached and drawn up by the pall bearers.

The other principal errand of the lorries was to bring in goods for the black market. In Changi it had been chiefly operated by Europeans, but at Sime Road the Eurasian Jews were the most important dealers. The Japanese took part in this racket too. The camp dealer paid his particular Japanese backer $1,000 in return for which he was allowed to send a lorry into town to buy whatever could be found. This was then sold to the internees for ten or twenty times what had been paid for it, and the dealer and the Japanese divided the profits.

There was another racket which consisted of cashing cheques drawn in English pounds for Japanese Occupation dollars, the only available currency. Japanese currency depreciated continuously during the last two years of the Occupation, partly through inflation by the Japanese themselves and partly because the Chinese circulated forged notes. The Japanese administration ordered more notes to be printed to meet their needs. The depreciation was so great that for some months before the surrender, an egg, which in normal times cost two cents, was sold for $25. The old rate of exchange between the pound and the dollar of course was quite unrepresentative of the value of the actual money under these circumstances, but though it was possible to obtain two and a half times the old rate, a fair exchange would have been more in the neighbourhood of twenty times.

One chief profiteer in both rackets was a Hindu Jew from Calcutta, named Mordecai. He came into the camp penniless in April 1943 and saved his evening bun every day for a month, selling it for a dollar. With the capital of $30 thus acquired, he started operations. He was so successful that he was reputed to have gone out of internment with a personal wealth of $80,000. If this sum is halved, allowing for the extravagance of camp rumour, he had still done pretty well. He was uneducated, and was unable to keep accounts, for which he employed a fellow-internee as secretary at $300 a month.

In March 1945, the number in the women's camp was more than doubled by the arrival of a fresh flood of internees, mostly Eurasians and Jewish. To accommodate them, a number of attap huts with mud floors had been built under Japanese direction. In addition, some men who lived near the women's camp had to vacate their huts for the newcomers and occupy new huts which had been built in the men's area. They also had to find accommodation in their camp for about 200 fresh men internees.

The new internees arrived on three different days. Officials of the men's and women's camps had been told to meet them and sort them out, while others were waiting to receive them in the huts where they were to live. Volunteers came to help them with their baggage. One of the porters was a Belgian whose French wife was a receptionist in one of the huts. He was a devoted husband and caused great confusion by taking every piece of baggage handed to him to the reception hut, so as to get a few words with his wife, irrespective of the destination of the baggage. All day long the rain poured and the new internees poured in with dripping clothes, soaking feet, and sheltering inadequately under broken umbrellas. The camp committee received them, sorting them into families, finding adoptive parents for lost babies and distributing them to appropriate huts.

Boys who arrived dressed in girls' clothes caused considerable confusion. The Japanese had been taking young boys for forced labour, and the mothers disguised them by dressing them as girls. This was not known in camp and a twelve-year-old, who claimed to be a boy but was wearing a girl's dress was bandied to and fro between the men's and women's authorities until in desperation, Miss Hegerty, the Women's Commandant, handed him over to a doctor to find out the truth.

Some of the new internees arrived in an under-nourished state, and many were sick. Part of a neighbouring hut had to be emptied to enlarge the hospital accommodation, and extra hospital staff had to be found. There were trained Eurasian nurses among the internees. Some joined the hospital staff while others attended to outpatients in the various huts. Some internees who were well off had been able to buy in the Singapore black market and were used to fairly good food. At first, they refused to eat the camp rations, throwing them into the drains and in buckets, which horrified us. Others were thankful to get regular meals of any kind.

Among the new internees was a stout, elderly, coal-black Tamil woman called Mrs. Begg. She had the remains of great beauty of an unusual kind. I nicknamed her the Black Greuze. Greuze is a 19th century French painter noted for his charming pictures of beautiful girls. She had a very violent temper and this, and the accompanying language, soon caused the Committee to move her from the hut to which she had been allocated and to give her a makeshift shack on the hillside near the hospital road. There she carried out chores, doing her washing, debugging her bed, in independence, and peaceable enough.

We had very interesting accounts of Japanese rule from these new internees, with their three years' experience of trying to remain alive. Many had had to work for the Japanese in offices, schools and other employment, as they had no other way of getting a living. They had all been compelled to learn a certain amount of Japanese. No lessons in the school might be given in English, and the small children were taught Japanese songs and what sounded like nursery rhymes which they used to sing in the camp. Everyone had to do a great deal of gardening and the poorer ones were half-starved, though the better-off and those who had had regular work looked quite well. Many people who could not get employment of any kind had to subsist by selling all their personal and household possessions, such as clothes, linen and furniture, on the black market. The alternative was to become a Japanese spy.

The espionage system was universal and no one was ever safe. Women were careful not to do their shopping from the same market or the same roadside merchants twice in a week, in case they should be reported for having too much money, with the implication that it came from England or China and that they must be English or Chinese agents. For the same reason, they did their marketing with covered baskets in case they should be reported for buying too much fish or meat at one time, these being most expensive luxuries. Stallholders were afraid of being reported for having too much to sell or for making too much money. Dog meat, cat meat and rat meat were all marked openly for sale in the markets. One family told me that they had to organise rat-hunts as it was impossible to keep a cat: they were always stolen for sale as meat in the markets.

The information collected by the spies was paid for according to a regular tariff. The highest price was paid for information against a Chinese, then against a Eurasian, while information against Indians or Jews received a relatively low reward. Anyone who was reported to the Kempeitai was arrested, which meant twelve or twenty-four hours without food, and probably a beating to start with. Then there would be an enquiry, perhaps with questioning by torture, and finally release, imprisonment or death.

It was a reign of terror, with the danger from spies so omnipresent that the new internees declared they almost found a compensation for being interned in the relative security of the camp. Some of these ex-spies were interned in March 1945. One of them was quite frank to me about her previous activities. They were not, however, interned in order to continue spying in the camp, but because the Japanese did not consider it safe to leave them at large. They were not anti-

British. They were weaklings in a difficult position, who wanted food and thought it safer to curry favour with tyranny, but it is hard to forgive the spies when one remembers into whose hands they delivered their victims.

The new internees were accustomed to working under Japanese orders. They took completely for granted one of the camp activities which had aroused our strongest protest—work in a military clothing factory which had been set up in the camp. In Changi, the Japanese set the whole women's camp by the ears by a demand that we should embroider thousands of the red stars which they wore on their uniforms to show length of service. We protested that this was war work and offered to make bandages instead, but we always received the same answer—the women "must volunteer" to do the stars. Eventually some did the work as the Japanese seemed determined. They were afraid of reprisals on the camp if it was not done, but the majority, though perhaps profiting by this, continued to disapprove.

In Sime Road, a match factory was started where most of the work was done by some Eurasians, who secured a small business in matches, which otherwise were unobtainable, by stealing and selling them in the camp. Finally, the Japanese started their biggest effort of the kind, a military clothing factory employing over a hundred women. A very strong, though polite, protest was put in by our camp about this, rather against the advice of the men who considered it was both useless and dangerous. The protest was in vain. Hut space was taken for the workrooms, sewing machines were installed, internee forewomen were appointed from among the friends of the Comfort Girls, and inducements to join the factory were offered in the shape of extra rations, slightly higher pay than that given for camp chores, and opportunities to buy luxuries like extra coffee, eggs and sugar. The majority of the Englishwomen refused to have anything to do with the factory, and continued to carry out the essential camp chores from which the factory employees were exempt. A few joined it either because they could not bear the hunger which was universal, or because they had children and wanted the chance to get extra food for them.

It was a very sore point with the Japanese that the English would not make uniforms for them but they took reprisal on one hut only. This was the hospital staff hut. Only one woman helped in the factory only on alternate weeks, as she had to continue her work as hospital cleaner or leave the hut. The Japanese realised that opposition in this hut was especially vigorous, and finally decided to take action. On the Thursday before Easter, Blue-Stockings stopped for a chat with one of the factory workers.

"Ah," he said "you are one of our friends! There are some people who will not be friends with us but they will be sorry for it." He then waved his stick towards the hospital staff hut on the opposite hill. "The people there are very *sombong* (stuck up) but we will show them that we can be more *sombong* still."

On Easter Monday they sent a gang of gardeners to dig up the staff hut's private gardens. We called ourselves Bukit Sombong (Proud Hill) after that incident.

Even with the willing workers they had difficulties. One of the forewomen complained loudly, "I shall have to sack Mrs. A. She's a perfect fool. She's been five days working on one shirt, and now she's brought it to me with one sleeve sewn into the neck and the other upside down!"

The material for the shirts was mostly the very poorest cotton. For knitting stockings, sweaters, and body-belts of which they were very fond, they had most beautiful quality Paton & Baldwin's wool, stolen we presumed out of Red Cross parcels. This wool was sometimes stolen by the factory workers and given to non-workers who knitted it into socks for the men internees.

In April 1945, the Japanese really began to believe that they could not hope to win the war. Whatever the reason, we were suddenly told that we were each to receive a whole Red Cross parcel to ourselves. The excitement cause by the announcement was tremendous. The camp could talk of nothing else for the three weeks which elapsed before the promise was fulfilled. We had received some parcels at Christmas 1943. Each had to be divided among seven people. Some bulk stores, consisting chiefly of cocoa, marmite and sugar, were received in September 1942. Otherwise nothing from the Red Cross had been allowed to reach us. The excitement caused on these two previous occasions, while we were still able to feed ourselves comparatively well, was nothing to the anticipation roused when our food was both scanty and disagreeable. To make things more thrilling, the parcels were of three different kinds, British, Canadian and American. Samples of each were opened in advance by the men, and their contents and relative value in calories and protein were assessed and published in typed notices. This added to the interest, and people spent hours trying to decide which kind they preferred.

The long delay before the parcels were given out made us think they were being withheld on purpose to tantalise us. Perhaps it was all a hoax and we were not going to get them after all. They were released at last. The Americans and Canadians in the camp were given their appropriate parcels, lots were drawn for the surplus, and everyone else got British. When we got our parcels, no one worried about vitamins or calories any more. At last we had some real, homely, honest English food: the very sight of the tins with their familiar names was romantic. All we could talk of was which we liked best, tinned bacon or delicious tinned puddings; tinned butter or condensed milk. The black market received a great impetus from the arrival of the parcels, and there was also an immense barter trade. The Jews, for example, had no use for the bacon, which was one of the most popular items with the Gentiles. Some people made wonderful bargains.

It became more and more evident that the Japanese were preparing for something. They took great gangs of men to dig horseshoe-shaped tunnels through the hills both within the camp and outside. We could see other gangs digging similar tunnels outside the camp. All kinds of rumours went round as to the purpose of these tunnels, since no one had ever seen anything like them or could imagine what they could be used for. We thought they were probably air-raid shelters for the Japanese camp officials, or possibly for us, though the latter did not square very well with their usual policy. A horrible story was circulated that in Manila the Japanese had shut their prisoners up underground and then poured petrol on them and set them alight.

This caused some alarm, but on reflection, it seemed a very roundabout way to get rid of us, and also rather expensive, as the diggers received extra rations. We remained in the dark as to the purpose of the tunnels until after liberation, when we were told that they were part of the defensive tactics which the Japanese used everywhere. They filled the tunnels with soldiers, all of whom had to be killed before the tunnel and the hill above it could be taken—a long and expensive business.

Our own A.R.P. consisted, on paper, of an elaborate organisation of stretcher-bearers, aid-posts and fire-fighters, and in practice of some open roofless slit trenches and a hopeful trust in Providence. We knew that if Britain had to fight to regain Malaya, it was very unlikely that we should be there to see the victory. Apart from the bombs and shelling, inevitable in an invasion, the Japanese could hardly have afforded to keep alive more than 30,000 P.O.W. in Changi Gaol alone, and thousands of civilian internees who all knew the country well, and many of whom had great influence and close relationships with the local people. It was quite obvious that the Japanese were preparing to fight over the whole of Singapore island if they fought at all, and as they could not send us to Malaya, the most probable solution to the prisoner problem appeared to be to machine-gun the lot.

Internment, July 1945

Three and a half years of it—and another day over,
The sun had gone down in a jumble of brilliant light:
The rose and the blue, the green and the gold have faded forever,
The startling moon turns the black asphalt white.

All is ethereal now in the ghostly silver,
It makes me restless, stirring the heart in me:
Memory, sorrow and hope are blent in fever:
Begone, O Moon, to your rest, and let me be.

The moon dazzles, the stars are dim beside her:
Too strange and lovely those white, enchanted beams.
I cover my eyes that my thoughts may wander wider,
Soothing despair with memories, hopes and dreams.

11 Farewell Syonan, Hello England

On the evening of 15 August 1945, an extraordinary rumour began to circulate in the camp. It concerned the collapse of Japan and some unheard-of catastrophe, bombing on a scale unknown before, which had brought it about. We dared not trust the rumours. We had heard too many, all too tantalising. We waited for the Sunday Meeting to get more definite news. We received confirmation, however, earlier still. The food fatigue brought our breakfast, not rice gruel this time but fried cakes of rice with a V for Victory stamped on each one. We knew then that something tremendous had really happened, since the cooks would never have dared to use the V sign without being very sure of themselves. At the Relatives' Meeting in the afternoon, we heard that Japan had actually surrendered and that there was a new weapon, the atom bomb, by which the surrender had been won. But inexpressibly relieved and delighted as we were to hear of victory at last, we could not help having a sense of awe and horror at the means of winning, and we asked ourselves whether any end could justify such means.

When we got back to camp after the meeting, we still did not dare to discuss openly what we had heard, but exchanged views privately in whispers, for so far there had been no confirmation of the surrender from the Japanese. As the days went by and our position remained ambiguous, many people began to grumble and protest. Urgent notices came from our camp officials imploring everyone to maintain camp discipline and carry on with work as usual, and above all to do nothing to provoke an incident. The Japanese were obviously in an uncertain frame of mind, sulky and inclined to burst into tears, but they were still plainly in control. They had handed the key of the rice store to our Quartermaster who had immediately trebled the rice ration. However, roll-call took place every day as usual.

We learned that though Japan had capitulated, General Itagaki, commanding in Malaya, had not decided whether to join in the surrender or to continue fighting on his own. This state of things continued for a fortnight. At last, he reached a decision. We only knew what this was when four British paratroops, Red Devils in beret and battledress, suddenly appeared in camp.

Syonan-to (Singapore) was re-taken by six paratroopers who landed on one of the airfields. Some of these immediately came to the internees' camp. I was in bed in hospital with a septic foot when this happened. In the middle of the afternoon rest hour, there was a bustle outside the hut. Then there was a sound of footsteps and strange voices on the verandah. Dr. Hopkins came in followed by the paratroopers, bursting with health and energy. We had seen nothing like them for years. They breezed rapidly down the ward and out again to complete their tour of the camp. The patients lay back and gasped and wondered what it meant and what would happen next. They were so full of life and enthusiasm that we half expected to see them leapfrog over the beds out of sheer high spirits as they passed. They had every reason in the world to be cheerful!

As soon as they left the hospital, they were mobbed by crowds of women demanding news. They received assurances that all was well and that we should be sent home to our families as soon as possible. After this, events moved rapidly. To patients tied by the leg in hospital, it was extremely tantalising to see people going freely to and fro between the two camps and making excursions to the town, and to be unable to attend the ceremony of hoisting the Union Jack in the camp, where God Save the King was sung by internees for the first time since our surrender. A wireless was put up for a few evenings just outside the hospital. When that familiar tune came over the air and we felt what it stood for—above all for liberty—it seemed to be the symbol of all we most desired.

People began to clamour to be sent home. Some of them believed that a fleet of luxury liners ought to have been assembled, as by a wave of the hand, to take them to whatever part of the world they wanted to go. I was determined to stay till I got some definite news of my family, one brother having been sent by the Japanese to work in Thailand while the eldest was serving in India and might possibly be sent with troops to Singapore. The camp gradually emptied and the camp hospitals were closed. Cases which could not be discharged or sent off immediately on a hospital ship were sent to the Singapore General Hospital, which had been re-opened under the supervision of Army nursing sisters. The last ten days in camp were so crowded with events and new sensations that they were almost exhausting.

Visitors flocked into the camp. First there were P.O.W. from Changi and other military camps. Husbands came over every day to see their wives, some joined by sons who had arrived with the liberating forces. Innumerable friends came to see us and gave us accounts of the facts about conditions in Thailand and the fate of friends and relations there. The horror of these stories heard at first-hand exceeds anything that can be conveyed in print. In a letter from home, I learnt that my P.O.W. brother was no longer in Thailand, having been sent to Japan

TO ALL ALLIED PRISONERS OF WAR

THE JAPANESE FORCES HAVE SURRENDERED UNCONDITIONALLY AND THE WAR IS OVER

WE will get supplies to you as soon as is humanly possible and will make arrangements to get you out but, owing to the distances involved, it may be some time before we can achieve this.

YOU will help us and yourselves if you act as follows :—

(1) Stay in your camp until you get further orders from us.

(2) Start preparing nominal rolls of personnel, giving fullest particulars.

(3) List your most urgent necessities.

(4) If you have been starved or underfed for long periods DO NOT eat large quantities of solid food, fruit or vegetables at first. It is dangerous for you to do so. Small quantities at frequent intervals are much safer and will strengthen you far more quickly. For those who are really ill or very weak, fluids such as broth and soup, making use of the water in which rice and other foods have been boiled, are much the best. Gifts of food from the local population should be cooked. We want to get you back home quickly, safe and sound, and we do not want to risk your chances from diarrhoea, dysentry and cholera at this last stage.

(5) Local authorities and/or Allied officers will take charge of your affairs in a very short time. Be guided by their advice.

Reproduction of the Surrender Notice.

IN accordance with the terms of the surrender of all Japanese forces signed by His Majesty the Emperor the war has now come to an end.

These leaflets contain our instructions to Allied prisoners of war and internees whom we have told to remain quiet where they are.

Japanese guards are to ensure that the prisoners get these leaflets and that they are treated with every care and attention. Guards should then withdraw to their own quarters.

Reverse Side of the Surrender Notice.

a year ago. The convoy in which he sailed was torpedoed and out of 2,000 prisoners only 650 were saved, of whom he was one. It was most interesting to compare notes of experiences with these P.O.W. visitors, and to hear their views on the fall of Malaya and on the behaviour of the Japanese. Nearly everyone who had lived for any length of time in Malaya before the capitulation was anxious to return, an attitude which was incomprehensible to the soldiers who had only known it during a few weeks or days of fighting, and after that as prisoners.

Numbers of local people came to visit the camp, nurses came to see the sisters and matrons, pupils to see their teachers, and servants to visit their old employers. Cheng Ah Moy suddenly turned up at the hospital one morning and I sat and talked to him on the verandah for some time. At first, he was quite overcome and went away round the corner of the hospital for some minutes to hide his tears. He was very thin but very clean and tidy, dressed in clothes too big for him and obviously borrowed. He enquired anxiously when my brother would be coming back and whether I could give him work. His family members were still alive and I could imagine how he had struggled to keep them so. I gave him a cup of tea, $150 in Japanese notes which was all I had, and a cake of fried rice. The money was almost worthless and did not give him much pleasure, but the rice cheered him up a little.

Many of these visitors brought us presents of food and clothes which probably they could ill afford. Dr. Williams' Malay boy and his wife and son came to see her one day, with many expressions of joy. Next day, the man came again with a big meal of cooked food and a quantity of eggs. He said that when they got home, his wife had wept because the Missy was so thin and ill, and had cooked and sent the food to help her to get strong again.

Hawkers came to the camp, mostly selling fruit and eggs. Many of them had little Chinese flags decorating their bicycles or baskets. I tried to buy one of these from a man as a souvenir, but he was so pleased at being asked for it that he would not take any payment. We had plenty of food, including a good deal of rice. We gave what was left over from our meals to women and children who came every day with baskets lined with leaves to collect scraps. Our food was a curious mixture of rice, vegetables, tinned meat and fruits provided by the Army, chocolate distributed by the Red Cross and by British sailors, and bread baked by the cooks of H.M.S. *Sussex* and sent to the camp every day.

We were also given quantities of English cigarettes. Those of us who had no money used them to barter with the hawkers. Every woman received a large gift parcel from the Australian Red Cross, a wonderful present which contained nearly every small oddment one could want, from toothpaste, safety pins and a thimble to writing paper, knitting wool, a brush and comb and a Penguin book to read on the voyage home. The parcels were extraordinarily well contrived. They were almost as varied and individual as children's Christmas stockings and were nearly as much fun to unpack. I hope the woman who planned them received on O.B.E. at least. She deserved it as much as anyone could for the sympathetic imagination she put into her work.

The smallest things amused us and gave us pleasure—to have proper soap again, and real face flannels: cotton which was not unravelled from an old sheet; combs and unrusted needles. We were peculiarly rich in toothbrushes and face flannels. At every turn, these useful articles were showered on us. We knew we should never find anything like it and we enjoyed it to the utmost while it lasted. It was like recovering from an illness and having a perpetual Christmas party.

On the afternoon of 11 September, some friends and I went into the town by taxi to attend the thanksgiving service at St. Andrew's Cathedral. On the way, we stopped for a moment to look at the

Y.M.C.A. building in Stamford Road where the Kempeitai had their headquarters. We looked at the cell where Dr. Williams, with two Chinese coolies and a Japanese sentry, had spent her first night in the Kempeitai's hands, hearing all night long the screams of people who were being tortured in the rooms overhead. The only sign of life remaining was the bugs crawling on the walls. We went out again and reached the Cathedral. It was packed, mostly with local-born men, women and children of all classes. The service was conducted by Bishop Wilson, Dr. Amstutz of the American Mission, and one Tamil and two Chinese priests, speaking their own languages. Afterwards I was greeted by a Tamil schoolgirl who had been in my class before the war.

Another young Eurasian girl had already been to see me in hospital twice. The second time, she brought me a present of a pineapple. I had had news of other pupils from a Jewish internee who had also been in my class, Rachel Elias. On arrival, she had gone round the camp with a smile on her face because she was at last reunited with her fiancé, who had been brought in two years earlier. She had also given me a dress, in compassion of my ragged state, and a petticoat which I slept in, having no night attire left.

The kindness of our friends among the local people and their happiness in meeting us and seeing us at liberty again was quite unexpectedly eager, and exceedingly touching. Taxis were placed at our disposal free of charge, and many internees were given clothes and shoes. There was an extraordinary atmosphere of happiness shared between East and West which was quite unlike ordinary times and events. We were no longer a race apart, but friends who with friends had endured a common suffering.

That evening, two friends and I had our first civilised meal for more than three and a half years, in the Officers' Mess of the Punjabi Regiment which had been the first to take over duty in Singapore.

The Colonel was an Indian, the other officers being both Indian and English. It was a wonderful evening, partly from the conversation of our hosts and partly from the sheer pleasure and excitement of actually dining out like civilised people again.

We were amused to see the number of tablets and pills they had to take, vitamin tablets, mepacrine tablets, all of them compulsory under severe penalties by army regulations. They gave us turkey from the Singapore Cold Storage, where apparently it had been stored for the last three and a half years. They were extremely proud because they had had a special compliment from Lord Louis Mountbatten on their smartness on guard the previous day when he landed, and because their Colonel had been chosen to represent the Indian Army at the ceremony of the Japanese surrender the following day.

This took place within the Municipal Building, a huge place facing the Padang, a large green field in the heart of town. Sister Clark and I went together to this surrender ceremony. We found places standing on a table on the Municipal Building verandah among a crowd of ex-P.O.W., both English and Indian. We watched the coming and going of officers in every sort of uniform for about two hours before Lord Mountbatten arrived. The whole of Singapore seemed to be there to rejoice at this, the positively final appearance of the Japanese. Incidentally, it was also the first appearance of any Japanese at any big ceremony in Singapore. They had never ventured to hold any sort of victory parade or demonstration themselves. On the Padang, sailors from the *Sussex* formed a great square within which were drawn up detachments of soldiers from the various regiments. The sailors from the *Richelieu* stood at one side, and every now and then immense aeroplanes roared overhead.

The great crowd waited patiently and expectantly. Suddenly from our right, out of sight, there was an outburst of angry yells and jeers from the crowd. A few moments later six Japanese Generals, followed by a secretary carrying a despatch case, came in sight. They had an escort of British, Australian and Indian soldiers who walked in open formation so that the prisoners could be clearly seen. The generals were in uniform, very spick and span, and they carried themselves straight and stiff. We respected the way in which they faced the ceremony of defeat.

The ceremony had of course been planned to humiliate them. From the behaviour of our camp guards under defeat, we knew how great the humiliation must be. If the generals had carried swords, we would have expected them to kill themselves on the long flight of steps which they had to climb, up to the entrance of the room where they were to sign the instrument of surrender. They climbed the steps without glancing right or left, holding themselves stiffly erect.

A couple of young ex-P.O.W. officers standing just behind us commented, "I say, you know, we shouldn't have done this."

"No, we shouldn't. It isn't cricket. No, it isn't cricket."

The Japanese Generals, in spite of everything, had sympathisers among those who also knew defeat.

For half an hour we waited for them to come out and at last they reappeared. They still tried to move with military smartness and uprightness, but the long business of signing the various papers had evidently broken their spirit. Their shoulders sagged and they did not move steadily. It was clear that they really felt they were beaten men, and strangely enough, I felt much less sorry for them. They went back by the road they had come and when they reached the corner leading to the docks, just out of sight, a great roar and snarl of rage went up from the Chinese standing there. It was a sound packed with three and a half years of accumulated hatred. Hardly any of the ex-prisoners whom I met took much interest in the judicial proceedings against the Japanese. The idea of personal revenge sickened us, and we were indifferent to punishment, retribution and justice. All we wanted then was not to come in contact with any Japanese ever again.

Later, at the trial in Singapore of Japanese war criminals, three of those who had been in charge of our camp were sentenced to death. All were reprieved following representations from many ex-internees including Dr. Williams and myself, who thought the death sentence was too severe a reprisal. It was commuted to ten years' imprisonment, of which those so condemned served seven, while lesser sentences were proportionately commuted.

After the ceremony was over, Sister Clark and I went to the back of the building to look for a lorry to take us to the camp. As we walked along, we heard a tremendous roar of cheering behind us, and the next moment we were engulfed in a seething whirlpool of Chinese, all half mad with joy over a young Chinese general who was walking among them. He had been on guard with guerilla troops inside the building during the surrender ceremony. On emerging he had been mobbed by the wild crowd. We stood and watched him pass, bowing and smiling to all and sundry. As the backwash of the mob disappeared, we hurried across the street and climbed into a lorry full of internees returning to Sime Road.

On the following evening, Lord Louis Mountbatten visited the camp to explain the difficulties which had delayed repatriation a little. He told us about the war in Burma and the general situation in the East and also an amusing story about the Japanese surrender in Burma.

"Your honour," wrote the Japanese general, "I am sending to offer you my surrender together with all the troops I have with me, and I shall at once give the order to surrender all my other units, if your honour will be so kind as to tell me where my units are!"

BY AIR MAIL.

THE STRAITS TIMES.
THE STRAITS TIMES.
THE SUNDAY TIMES.
SINGAPORE FREE PRESS.
THE STRAITS BUDGET.
STRAITS TIMES ANNUAL.

Telephone 5471 (5 lines)
Cables: Times Singapore

THE PREMIER NEWSPAPERS OF EASTERN ASIA CIRCULATING THROUGHOUT
MALAYA, BORNEO, SIAM, JAVA, SUMATRA.

INCORPORATED IN THE
STRAITS SETTLEMENTS

HEAD OFFICE:
140-146, CECIL STREET
SINGAPORE

November 3, 1946.

Miss M.Thomas,
c/o Mrs. Milton,
St.Paul's Rectory,
Westgate, Lincoln,
ENGLAND.

Dear Madam,

In reply to your letter of Oct.9, I regret that we are unable to supply back numbers containing reports of the Sime Road trial.

Tominaga, Kawazai and Kobiyashi were sentenced to death by the War Crimes Court. Suzuki was sentenced to life imprisonment and Myamoto to eight years.

On revision by the G.O.C. -- following many protests by ex-internees -- the death sentences were reduced to ten years imprisonment, and the other sentences reduced accordingly.

Yours faithfully,

G. L. Peet.

(G.L.Peet)
Assistant Editor.

GLP/PJE.

Reply to the author's enquiry.

At the end of his speech, Lord Mountbatten signed autographs for at least twenty minutes. Some of these were sold by enterprising internees that same evening for $100 each. In the middle of the autograph session, the eldest Iraqi woman arrived and pressed breathlessly forward into the crowd.

"The money! The money! Where is he changing the money?" she cried. Miss Hegerty assured her that no money was being changed.

"But is he not changing the Japanese money?" cried the Iraqi. "What did he come for then?"

The Iraqis had saved a handsome sum of Japanese money which they had earned by boiling water for other internees on illicit fires at $7 a kettle. It took a good five minutes to persuade her that the liberator of Singapore was not personally changing the worthless Japanese currency for the new dollar notes.

The Japanese currency was abolished. The former Straits dollar currency was recognised at its full face value, on a level with the new currency which was at once issued. This was unfortunate as the old Straits currency had mainly accumulated in the hands of friends of the Japanese, who had held onto it more and more tightly as the Japanese currency depreciated and the failure of Japan became more certain. They were therefore quite well off, while other people had to wait till they could earn or somehow acquire the new currency.

The numbers in camp were by this time much reduced and more were leaving daily. Some who were staying on to help identify Japanese officials who had gone into hiding, or to see old colleagues and friends in the town, had gone out of camp to live in Singapore. It was a curious glimpse into the nature of human feelings. As the camp was breaking up and friends were parting, many people were unhappy. Of course they longed to go home and were delighted to be free. Of course they hated the memory of internment—but still it had not been entirely bad.

Women, more than men, take root in the present whatever that present may be, and the disturbance of the roots is painful. In our case, the roots were three and a half years old and they had flowered into loyal friendships, in much that was arresting, new and strange, and in a life permeated with an extraordinary sense of community and of closely-knit fellowship. We had shared with one another a unique experience. With liberation, we had to face a new and puzzling world where at first we would be complete strangers.

Nobody, however sympathetic, would be quite able to grasp the implications of the stories we told them, or see the funny side of what we laughed at, or to realise any of the intangible things which must be left unsaid. It was still very strange to be free, to be one's own master, to have liberty of choice, and not to bear the daily responsibility of playing one's part, however insignificant it might be, in a communal life against heavy odds. We were individuals again and it was difficult to get used to it. At any rate, whatever the reason, people looked sad as well as happy, and some said goodbye with tears.

On Tuesday, 18 September, I left the camp with twenty-two other women and three children to go on board the *Nieuw Holland*, a Dutch boat. We had a considerable amount of luggage. In addition to the personal possessions and relics of internment which we wished to take with us, we had been issued with a kit-bag each and a supply of army equipment for the voyage.

That journey home, our first real and close contact with the outside world, was something which could never be forgotten. Everybody was so amiable, kind and considerate! Everyone was interested, polite, gentle, helpful and charming.

In camp, behaviour had for so long been that of people whose nerves were strained to the last degree that we had forgotten anything else existed, and this was like walking into a new world. We could not think we had done anything to deserve such treatment. It must be due to the essential goodness of human nature, something in which for a long time it had grown almost impossible to believe. Yet it was not quite true that in camp, when pushed to extremity, selfishness and self-preservation, not social feeling, had sometimes shown themselves as the basic forces in human nature. The very women who were cruelly hard, critical and grasping in competition with any, even the old or sick who interfered with their chances of survival, would not lift a finger to do the Japanese work which would have gained them extra rations and other privileges.

We reached Colombo and entered the harbour to a welcome of hooting ship's sirens, shouting crews and flying bunting. We could not believe it was all on our account, and indeed it was not. We were more than merely ourselves, we were a symbol of victory and the end of the War. On shore, we were greeted by the band of an Indian regiment playing on the quay and by hundreds of Women's Royal Naval Service members (Wrens) who took us to the Echelon Barracks and gave us whatever we required, from a hot bath, a hair shampoo and a face massage, to a cup of tea, magazines, shoes and an outfit of civilian clothes. They were so kind, patient, friendly and polite. I think some of the long bitterness of internment began to wear away at Colombo.

It took a long time after repatriation for a sort of amazement at people's gentle manners and kindly ways to pass off. We marvelled at their ways for Britons had been hideously bombed, and rationed, and had stood day after day in endless queues, and for six exhausting years had borne the burden of a tremendous war. They might well have been excused for being irritable or peevish. We felt we had come back to a very wonderful nation.

On the way to England we called at Port Suez, where we were fitted with clothes for a cold climate. These were provided by branches of the Red Cross in Canada, Australia and the United States, and by the Lord Mayor's Fund. We were exceedingly glad to receive these warm outfits. We landed at Liverpool on 16 October in a fog and in the middle of a dock strike. The previous evening we had been given identity cards, railway vouchers, application forms to Government for compensation and other papers. A charming Red Cross representative brought our letter and seemed much struck by our appearance in our Port Suez outfits.

"Why" she asked presently, "are you all wearing such funny clothes?" We replied that we rather fancied our clothes and asked what was wrong with them. She only smiled.

A huge crowd had stood at the quayside all day to welcome us. The fog had delayed the ship for nearly twelve hours but the people had remained standing in the cold until we arrived. Even then, at four o'clock in the afternoon, they were not allowed on board. They waited until it was nearly dark, shouting greetings to their friends and relatives on deck, while speeches of welcome to the P.O.W. were made by representatives of the fighting services. The P.O.W. went ashore that evening to transit camps. The civilian ex-prisoners remained on the ship till the next morning. After breakfast at 6 a.m., they went ashore to catch the various trains. It was with a curious feeling, half unreal, half puzzled, that one stepped onto English ground after six years. The Liverpool Customs shed and Liverpool railway station are not the most beautiful buildings in the world, but grey, grimy and severely useful as they are—how very English! There were hoardings with familiar advertisements.

We looked about us to see if the War had changed England a great deal, but it seemed much the same. People smiled a welcome to us as we passed.

We waited a long time for the London train. I went to the station bookstore and indulged myself by buying five different newspapers and periodicals: *The Manchester Guardian, Time and Tide, The Spectator, The New Statesman,* and *The Soviet Weekly*. Someone else had *The Times*. Another had *The Mirror* and someone bought *The Express*, so we were well supplied. I tried to buy *Theatre World* but it was sold out and when I did get a copy some days later, I was disappointed to find how much it was changed, reduced by paper rationing to the size of *Lilliput*. Minute by minute, we explored and assimilated the world to which we had come back, like Rip van Winkles waking out of dreams. We sat on piles of luggage and read our papers. When the train came, we scrambled for seats in the packed coaches. We enquired about lunch but the seats were all booked and we could get nothing till we reached London at three o'clock in the afternoon.

As the train left the urban districts and travelled among the autumn landscape, I stared at the extraordinary beauty of English trees. An atmosphere of strangeness and unreality still hung about everything, as though events could still be sudden and unexpected and life insecure. Nothing seemed normal or safe to count on and none of us knew our way about this England, which one instinctively felt must have greatly changed during six years of war.

Presently we were travelling through the outskirts of London, past brick walls, neatly kept hedges and gardens, and occasional gaps among the buildings where a bomb had fallen. We entered Euston, drew up at a crowded platform, and streaming from our carriages found ourselves swept away from one another and engulfed in a swirling crowd of strangers. For a moment, London itself, unchanged, massive, respectable as ever, filled both mind and eye, and from distant streets the homely sounds of London traffic roared about us.

To my great relief, I was met by my aunt who found me among the clamouring crowd. She embraced me warmly with cries of joy and began to make plans for getting to her flat.

"I suppose you haven't got any luggage, you poor darling?" she asked.

"I've got a lot of luggage," I answered with pride. "The Red Cross gave us quantities of things. Look at these clothes I'm wearing."

My aunt stepped back to get a good look at me, and a moment later peals of joyful laughter rang out. Nobody took any notice however, as there were at least 200 other ex-internees, all looking equally quaint. In any case, I had forgotten for the time being what it was to be embarrassed by appearances.

It was not till I had been back in England for some weeks that I began to realise what repatriation, victory and the end of the war meant. I looked at the blue and green hills, wide and calm and peaceful, with the grey walls meandering over them and the narrow brown hedges, and thought how small a country England was compared with her great Empire, and above all compared with the territories of her enemies. Standing almost alone, England had first held those enemies in check, and then with her Commonwealth and her other allies had beaten them. It was a thought of sobering exaltation.

I have listened to people who wring their hands over victories and cry that in war no one is victorious. Such people do not know what they are saying. I had seen a victorious enemy lording it and swaggering in the homes of my friends, and I had been a prisoner in a country where the people of my race had been the undisputed rulers. It is not what one has gained that counts at the end of a war: it is the things one has not lost.

This small country had borne the greatest burden of all in the long and weary war. Her people were my people, and I felt an infinite pride in being one of them. It was the most wonderful experience to listen to people in England talking casually of that crucial period when Germany sat waiting at their very doorstep liable at any moment to walk in. I had seen invasion and what it could do. It was infinitely reassuring to know that here at home there was no flight and no panic, and that in war the English were as firm and solid and sensible as they were in peace.

People often want to know if we got any good out of internment. "Did you gain anything from it?" they ask. Of course. I learnt drawing and French and found time to read and assimilate books which I could never have dealt with in ordinary life. Many people made lifelong friendships and some felt they had established a very deep and lasting tie of unity and affection with the people of Singapore.

It seems that there are three things in life which count more than anything towards happiness. These are: not to lose your self-respect under any circumstances, to have enough to eat, and to have friends. The two things essential for success in life are courage and mercy. The two qualities without which life is not worth having at all are truth and affection. Those impressions were gathered out of a hotch-potch of strange experiences which upset most of one's previous simple notions as to the natures and intelligence of civilised human beings.

Finally, even when we felt down, when the faults and failings incidental to humanity got most unbearably on one's nerves, it was always possible to alter one's outlook by reflecting: "We're all in this by our own choice. We are bearing the same thing and we chose to face this life together. We could have gone but, for love of one thing or another, we stayed, because we wanted to." With this realisation there would come a sudden illumination of the mind, and a warming of the heart, and one could say simply and truly: "We few, we happy few, we band of brothers."

Always Exiled, Always at Home

Lovely the brilliant sun, the tempered breeze:
Not to this scented light my spirit cleaves,
But far, under leaden skies, to storm-dark trees.
O hills! O rain! O wind and lashing leaves!

In lands like Eden the exile yearns for home:
By sun-bright flowers she longs for Cotswold stones,
And I long, although through Paradise-lands I roam,
For the earth, the air, the water that made my bones.

What senseless spell compels me to wander away?
Why not settle at home in peace and be easy there?
There's a lure of promise that calls me always to stray,
Seeking for far wild mountains and alien air.

For the lights and colours and movement of different
   climes,
(Though underneath all things are always the same):
For the breathless wonder that catches my throat at
   such times.
I seek, I must go, I give praise, I am glad that I came.

Diary Written at Sime Road Camp
(Extracts)

Wednesday 5 July 1944

We have been here at Sime Road since 7 April. Most of the huts had names and inscriptions left behind by the P.O.W. The Sikh Quarters had "We are loyal to our King" (by the Italian Navy). Our hut had lists of dead, working in Thailand. Of one contingent 59 percent were dead: of 3,000 others 800 were dead. They went to Malaya in April last year to make a railway in the jungle. There was a list of causes of death: cholera, typhus, dysentery, beri-beri, ulcers and starvation. It is said the men were made to work while sick, until they dropped. Parr is dead. Francis is very fit but still in Thailand. Rycroft is in Sydney. Tom Cotterell is in Changi now and sent me $5.

Most people are much happier here than in Changi but some dislike it. The food is plentiful but totally lack quality. We get almost no protein. There is only milk for children under three. Two days ago the Nips took all the soya bean curd brought into our camp for the children. We have a regular weekly Relatives' Meeting from 3–4 on Saturdays: send parcels twice a week and write daily. We get a small sugar ration about once in ten days and a small quantity of *gula batu* or *gula malacca* is sold once in ten days. We live on rice and vegetables. There is a lot of palm oil in the diet and just now the rice is very good quality, under-milled and has polishings added to it. We get a bun (bread made of rice) every other day.

Two days ago some drunken sentries went into one of the men's huts and fell over a man and cursed and beat him up. Said we would "all be shot and have no food for three days". A complaint was made to their officer and next day an apology came from the sentries. They especially apologised to "those men who had never been drunk". The whole Camp was cleaned and the grass cut for inspection by a "very big General" last week. He came, glanced round and was gone in a few minutes.

Mrs. Begg is very troublesome. Blue-Stockings hit her yesterday and she is to have Mrs. Caalen's shack to herself. She was moved to the Iraqi's hut a few days ago from No. 5 using horrible language! Nabi stole her sugar, so she and the Iraqi had a fight. Dr. Hopkins is said to be furious because no one has proposed her as Camp No. 1. I am voting officer for Hut No. 11, the candidates are Mrs. Chowns and Mrs. Mather. Mrs. Mather has no chance.

Letters from home keep repeating that the Colonial Office says I am Organising Secretary of the Camp and that we are in "Changi Camp". Letters were written a year ago. They heard in May 1943 that I am safe, but nothing about Francis: were hoping for letters from Singapore by July last year. The Nips must have given some account of the Camp, allotting Lady Thomas some imaginary office, and then muddled my name with hers. Many people will be very jealous!

Slit trenches are to be dug in case of air-raids. The Nip officers have each one funk-hole.

Much of the Camp is beautiful, the trees, the open places, the hillsides outside. I have made a stool under a bush with a view across to a Chinese *kampong* in trees on the hill opposite and another hill with a Chinese graveyard to the right.

The Camp is full of rats. We are not troubled with them so much as other huts are, especially the Sikh hut where they are very bold. Hut No. 10 had a lot of disturbances which sounded like a poltergeist. People said it was a monkey. The nuns sprinkled holy water and said prayers in the end and the disturbances ceased, so very likely it was a poltergeist or something of the sort. They always occurred directly after lights out, with no visible agent. One or two snakes have been killed, harmless ones I believe. The children are very cruel to crickets and lizards which they call "blood-suckers". They also steal fruit a great deal.

Mrs. Bateman has her drawing class on Monday evenings in the rambutan grove where we have the Church of England services. The Bishop officiated early Mass last Sunday. He looks thin and worn but very cheerful. He is said to have been badly tortured while outside the Camp. We have a weekly concert with the men's orchestra, which comes and plays on Saturday evenings outside the hospital, in front of our hut. This is called Piccadilly.

There was a lot of illness when we first came here, chiefly malaria and dysentery. This has improved but we still get malaria and a number of younger people are cracking up for want of protein. I am still well, thank goodness. I think we shall be here a long time.

Mrs. Begg's nickname is Annie Laurie. Joan Wight's summer house at No. 1 is known as "Comfort House". Anne MacDonald is christened "Mortuary MacDonald' by Mrs. Bentley.

The carpenters made me a very fine wooden bed. The cross boards are all fitted in loose so that they can be taken out to look for bugs, and it actually has a low back to it. I gave my "Chopped Ham and Eggs" invalid food in the Christmas parcel to Miss Stewart to give to Nicholson. The Nips (Blue-Stockings) have offered to supply chicken for Mrs. Shelton-Palmer at $19 a kati. Bentley collected from us this morning on behalf of Mrs. Mulvaney. I contributed 50 cents but shall not do so again.

Monday 10 July

I forgot the month, my first entry was wrongly dated June. Tania gave a party in Nellie's garden last night—vermicelli, savoury rice and a salad made of potato stalks, most of which I prepared. We had mint and chilli in the salad, it was good.

We had Relatives' Meeting and concert on Saturday. During the concert, eleven lorries containing Dutch and British troops went along the road and came back. They were bearded, dirty and looked as if they had just come from Malaya or Sumatra. They looked amazed to see us and some of them waved.

Biddy Bryant told us the story of the Bishop's imprisonment which her fiancé had told her. The Bishop and Yoxall were questioned about a very large sum of money which had been sent in secretly to the Bishop in Camp. The Japanese wanted to know what had become of it and suspected it had been used for seditious purposes in Singapore. The Bishop said he had no recollection whatever of receiving it but if he had received it, he had certainly paid it into the central fund. Examination of Yoxall's books showed no record of it. They were both tortured, but continued to deny all knowledge of the money. After some days, the Kempeitai man in charge of the torture said to the Bishop, "You know if you go on like this, you will die." The Bishop answered, "I have commended my soul to God, and I can only say that I know nothing about this money and I am telling the truth."

The man said to both of them. "You are both gentlemen. Gentlemen should not tell lies." They answered, "We have not told lies. We know nothing about this money."

The Kempeitai man said, "I believe what you say, and I can't go on with this. I shall have to resign."

He went to his superior and told him this. The Bishop and Yoxall were now put in a cell together for the first time. They discussed the matter thoroughly and were forced to conclude that the only possible explanation was that the doctor on the ambulance to whom the money had been handed had simply pocketed it. They did not see why they should lie to protect a thief (and such a thief), so eventually they told the Japanese of this. This doctor is now out with the Kempeitai. I don't know which it is. (Later—It was Boyer. He is dead now.) The disgusting way in which a number of the men doctors have behaved, their sheer blatant dishonesty and rottenness, makes one feel deeply horrified. Kate feels terribly ashamed of her profession in which such men are her superiors. A number of these men would be struck off the rolls by the B.M.A. "for conduct unbecoming a medical man" if the truth were known.

Saturday 15 July

Mrs. Shelton-Palmer is dying. All last night she was praying to die. She does not know that her son died in P.O.W. Camp. Seven men who were taken by the Kempeitai months ago have come back from Miyako. They include Hebditch, who is said to have had a frightful beating-up. Nothing about Mrs. Nixon. Mrs. Begg was put in a cell by the Nips for two days. She had to go to the lavatory in our Camp with Sikh escort. She said that there was a little hole in the corner of the room where she could perfectly well wee-wee there, and save all the walk up and down the hill. She has been examined by Home, and threatened with certification unless she behaves. She begged not to be send back to Miyako because the amahs beat her. However, I don't think she can behave.

The men fired the lallang in their Camp a few days ago under Nip orders, and it was a fine sight. We thought it was going to be dangerous but it was managed by planters who understand these things. There have been orders to burn the lallang for 100 yards round every hut. Slit trenches are being made everywhere and new bridges over the drains. Also holes dug to plant papayas, and large boulders prized out of the lower garden. We are told to make another road.

18 July 1944

Letter from Mother yesterday, dated 11 July last year. She still had no news of Francis. Drawing class yesterday disturbed by screams of children throwing stones at birds. Mrs. Begg stealing peasticks in order to knock down jambus with them, and Marcia and Mavis Seth taking a walk and talking rather crackpottedly as usual.

Thursday 20 July

Voting yesterday and today for Area Committee and Hut Superintendents. Hopkins on Committee and Major Grey on the Hill: our Hill, Helen Latta, unopposed. Began a picture in colours looking across to Chinese graveyard this morning, a young bamboo in front. Mended Philip's socks, had to patch, no darning wool and too fine to unravel.

Septic spot on my left ankle lanced yesterday: now practically healed. Weather very dry, fine and windy. Someone in the men's Camp died recently of malaria and typhus. Been reading *Artists in Crime* by Ngaio Marsh: one of the best detective stories I have read. Have had a lot of chillies from our chilli bush.

I put on weight on this diet but nearly all on abdomen and diaphragm: very annoying.

Friday 21 July

A very cold storm this morning. Yesterday a slight eclipse of the sun at 1.30. Everyone today wrapped in coats and blankets or getting into bed for warmth. In our big room with unshuttered windows both rain and wind blow in on a day like this. Not a pleasant foretaste of the rainy season. Reading *Travels with a Donkey*, by far the best book of its sort I have read; I suppose the prototype of all the more intimate travel books, certainly so of *The Path to Rome*.

At an interview with Mrs. Chowns and Weekly (heads of the Men's and Women's Camps respectively), the General (Saito) was asked yesterday to inquire after Mrs. Nixon. He rang up the Kempeitai in Singapore and was told "She is well, no cause for anxiety" and would be returned when the investigation was finished. This means that she is still alive, and not in Miyako. The General insists that all boys over ten must go to the Men's Camp. Hurrah! Hurrah!

Monday 24 July

Hugh Frazer and Alan Kerr back from Singapore today. Neither is very well. Frazer could walk with help, but Kerr had to be brought in on a stretcher.

We have voted recently as to which of two diets we prefer.

No. 1: rice and soup every tiffin, large bun or *nasi goreng* alternate evenings, with a small bun and *bubor* on Sundays.

No. 2: *nasi goreng* or soup and rice alternate days, soup and rice on Sundays for tiffin and large bun every evening with a spread if possible.

No. 1 diet won by a small majority, to the great disgust of most Europeans who wanted the daily bread. I voted for No. 1 because the bun is sometimes made the day before we get it, and is going sour when we have it: also I like soup every day.

A good deal of rain the last two or three days, very stormy. Two more bad cases of dysentery, Mrs. Attias and Mrs. Yonge, who was brought to the hospital on a stretcher this evening. The Medical Orderly came over with the husband this afternoon during the storm, got bored with the interview and suddenly appeared in the doorway of our dormitory and asked several times for Dr. Hopkins. Finally she sat up and he spotted her, pointing with outstretched arm and a cry of glee in her direction, and bustled off between our beds to her bedside. He gave her a cigarette and had about five minutes' chat, interlarded as usual with grunts. "*Hohr!*" (looking round the room at the recumbent forms all draped in blankets) "*Banyak Sejok! Hohr! Tidor! Hohr! Sakit?*" Mrs. Cornelius was sitting by her bed in her petticoat doing her nails when he arrived and she continued quietly to do so without putting on any more clothes.

Thursday 3 August

The engagement of Mrs. Ferroa (a Hut No. 1 Comfort Girl) to a Nip called Yamamoto was announced yesterday. There was a betrothal feast in the evening. Sensation!

Sullivan and Katey distressed because Ackers and Hopkins bully Mrs. Cornelius so badly. She was in tears yesterday both at lunch and supper-time apparently. Seeing her sitting alone after lights out, I asked her to come for a walk and we strolled along the road in the moonlight for twenty minutes.

Alan Kerr who came back from Singapore with Frazer also has gangrenous sores from lying on the ground and is very weak. The Married Men's Committee have put in a request that Mrs. Nixon should be brought back. The Men's Camp Committee had asked that a Nip M.O. should visit the prisoners in Singapore.

Found bugs in my bed two days ago—the first time. Washed and disinfected my bed, and think I have got rid of them.

Discontent about the distribution of pay. Mrs. Bales insisted on being paid for making her private garden and got away with it. Many jobs grossly overpaid: others underpaid by comparison.

The General came round the other day and was annoyed because we didn't bow properly and slapped Tominaga and Blue-Stockings for it. Now the sentries insist on bowing very strictly.

Monday 21 August

Have spent eight days in bed, four in hospital, owing to a boil on my right leg. Was discharged this evening. Philip came over this afternoon and told me about the theft of a man's money in his camp. He has to investigate it and thinks he has tracked down the thief. Says they are all feeling the diminution of our rations. The sacks of rice at present being issued at 7½ percent short. Quantities of rice are being brought into the Camp. Sometimes it is mixed with ground peanuts which is quite nice. There was an investigation into our food supply following complaints about our kitchen, and it was found to be 1 percent short. The men's, however, was 8 percent short.

The Nipponese have said that air raids are "absolutely imminent" (verbatim quotation).

Have had seven postcards since last entry: four from Mother, one from Father, one from Lambie and one from Dorothy May. David is in India. Christopher in Burma. Mother has had a card from Francis in Thailand—"very well". All at home well.

Friday 25 August

Sugar ration today. Made Philip some biscuits of pounded oven-dried rice *bubor*, palm oil and sugar. Blue-Stockings came round during Rest Hour the other afternoon to see about chicks. No one stood up as everyone was half-asleep and practically unclad. He went off in a rage muttering "*Sombong, banyak sombong*" under his breath and said that since we were so *sombong* we could do without chicks.

Next day, our fans were removed; we thought this was additional reprisals, but all the fans in the Camp, except the hospital and kitchen, are being taken away. Today he says we can have the roof mended but he has no *kajang* for chicks. Without chicks the rain blows in to the middle of the dormitory when it is raining. Last night very disturbed by machine-gun practice at intervals, and by snoring and the visitations of cats.

30 January 1945

Impossible to keep a regular diary owing to shortage of paper. I had malaria and was in hospital for ten days, discharged 21 December. Several raids, some clearly visible from Camp. Sisters go over, two together, to nurse in the men's hospital.

I have bought a paintbox for $30. Green chillis are sold eight for $1, Mrs. Deakes, the broker, taking 10 percent. Daily roll call has been instituted since 18 December except on Sundays. Some letters have been received, my most recent dated April 1944. Lady Thomas heard from Formosa, dated September 1944. *Gula malacca* is $34 a kati (prices all vary). Coffee at $45 per kati. Lots of palm oil again at $7 per half pint. Have read Boswell's *Life of Johnson* and Johnson's *Tour in the Hebrides*. Most of our Camp is now Camp garden, growing vegetables. The Nips steal our fruit regularly. All barbed wire removed round Camp, instead we have a board fence.

31 July 1945

A card dated Christmas 1944 came to me yesterday from my Father saying "Christopher killed in action. Don't grieve too much. He is safe and happy now. We are quite well. God keep us all. Dearest love." (Christopher was my youngest brother. He was twenty-five years old.)

Appendix

Extracts from
POW-WOW

MY STARS!
by
The Old Squaw

Motto for the Week:
Bright star! Would I were steadfast
as thou art

—John Keats

The Old Squaw had just been repatriated (to Changi) from Miyako, where she was sent in consequences of various mysterious symptoms, beginning in her teeth and extending to her feet, which had defied diagnosis by any of our physicians and even by the V.A.Ds and the Camp in general. The Old Squaw laid about her mightily with tongue and trompahs but the Housing Committee were too strong for her, and finally she retired in high dudgeon to roost under the roof-tree of the Red Cross Hut in a carefully slung hammock, with her belongings festooned from the cross-bars about her.

There was no one to be seen when I first visited the Hut so I stood in the middle of the floor and whistled. This produced a sudden commotion overhead and some impassioned mutterings, and a moment later the picturesque features of the Old Squaw became visible in the roof, peering down at me over the edge of her hammock like Socrates from his basket. It was no Socratic dialogue which followed however.

"Sit down! Sit down!" she cried, indicating a handy step-ladder as she spoke. "The Camp is a terrible state. I've worked out a whole lot of schemes for reform but my Changi memory is getting so bad that I'm afraid I shan't remember them much longer. What an age you've been coming to interview me! Always idle, I fear, and eating like a queue-marker all the same! Never there on time when wanted, but perpetually popping up under one's feet when least expected, like every other Camp pest! Well, well! Let's make the best of a bad job like Mrs. Nixon and carry on."

"It's this civil war," she explained in confidential tones as I settled down on my perch. "This feud between Officialdom and the Red Cross. The Camp's nerves won't stand much more of it. My idea is that each side should recruit as many supporters as possible, arm them with trompahs, bad eggs and coconuts, and settle the matter in an unfair fight in E Garden. By the time they've killed each other off there'll be plenty of room for the new internees, and thus the Camp's mind will be relieved on both these difficult questions."

"What about those of us who prefer a quiet life to all this fighting?" I asked, rather alarmed.

You can go to the boiler corner of A Garden—surely you'll be out of the way there all right—and play at Red and Black," she replied.

Of course I have not the slightest idea of what she meant by this, but I thought it best to change the subject in case it led to trouble.

"What do you think of the food just now?" I asked.

"Do you never think of anything but your stomach?" she asked tartly. "However, there's only one word to described the food. It begins with a B—and it isn't *bubor*."

The subject seemed to enrage her so much that I thought it best to defer my other questions to a more favourable moment. A last glance as I quitted the Garden showed the Old Squaw hanging from the roof by one foot like a wah-wah, and drinking about a gallon of tea which Mrs. Mulvaner had left for the builders. I admired her dexterity in being able to swallow upside-down, and recollected that this is a sure cure for the hiccups. I thought it might be a good idea if we started some training classes and lectures so that we could practise this useful accomplishment now.

* * * * *

3 *June 1942*

Personal Notes

If this rain goes on, the out-of-door sleepers may emulate the kitten that wandered up and down Tin Pan Alley looking for a comfortable place to sleep. It finally settled down in the crook of Mrs. Koek's leg where she found it to her surprise the following morning. Residents of E Lower be warned.

Surprising few casualties in the Keep Dry Rush, darkness and bad legs considered. Unfortunately Mrs. MacDonald landed in the drain and Miss Young's bed gave up the ghost. Too bad!

Don't know whether Irene Whitehad managed to keep dry. Bad luck being tied to bed and though we envy her for getting the fresh air we hope she will be given a bit more privacy, and more—that she will not need it too long, but soon be up among us again.

And with all the storms of passion that rage through the Camp, emotional anchors are needed. Our own choice is Mrs. Ferguson, who remains calm, level-headed and efficient regardless of the vicissitudes of our present life.

* * * * *

Committee Notes

- On 25 May we were informed by the Garrison Command that His Excellency Sir Shenton Thomas was permitted to rejoin his fellow internees. He is now accommodated in a comfortable part of the Men's Camp. The termination of his almost solitary confinement is hailed with great relief. No reason for this confinement has been given by the Japanese.

- On 27 May the Men's Camp was ordered to evacuate the hospital and transfer to the upper floor of the European Block at 24 hours' notice. (This refers to the women's hospital.) This meant the postponement of the General Meeting and great pressure of organisation and work on the shoulders of the Camp Executives. After long discussions with the Japanese authorities, and a memorandum submitted by the Medical Committee, the Garrison Commander finally agreed to the accommodation of the hospital on the ground floor of the European block.

  The next two days proved trying to the whole Camp but the great rearrangement of cells was managed at last and the hospital—now to be termed the sick bay—established in the room at the far end of the ground floor of E Block and the few adjacent cells.

- On Tuesday 26 May the Women's Camp had a great treat as a concert was organised for their benefit by the Men's Camp. The concert was held in the central courtyard. Lt. Okasaki attended and the women were allowed to sit round their side of the courtyard. It was a first class entertainment and we all thoroughly enjoyed it.

- We said good-bye to Mrs. Zehnder on Sunday 31 May with mixed feelings. We were delighted to see her released but she will be missed by our community. Those of us who started our internment in House A at Katong will never forget her kindness. Since coming to Changi, Mrs. Zehnder has been an elected member of the Executive Committee each month, and has continued to represent her floor whose interests she had much at heart.

* * * * *

Entertainment

Lack of space prevents our giving adequate appreciation of Mrs. Milne's last entertainment held almost a fortnight ago. Further words are not necessary: our applause indicated the extent of our approval and gratitude.

On Friday 5 June Mrs. Mike Kent will entertain at the piano. Further arrangements depend upon future black-out regulations.

* * * * *

10 June 1942

Committee Notes

Black-out time seems to vary considerably. At the time of writing it is 9.30 p.m. When the black-out is later than 8.30 p.m. the time for evening showers will automatically go back to 8.30–9.30 p.m.

The King's Birthday will be kept on Thursday 11 June

* * * * *

Library

Will borrowers from the Library please not keep their books for more than 4 DAYS as others are so often waiting for a particular book. Books can always be renewed for another period if required. A great number of borrowers have kept books for long periods and if this continues the librarians may have to start a system of fines to be paid into the Red Cross.

* * * * *

Letter

Dear Editor

When talks after black-out began, many people said, "What a splendid idea!" and the talks held outside in the Garden drew a large and attentive audience.

When the weather forced speakers and audience inside, the speaker found it difficult to make herself heard because of the noise inside and outside the Carpenter's Shop.

It is inevitable that in such a large community as this Camp, tastes differ considerably, and a talk that interests one person has no appeal for another, but surely it is not unreasonable to expect that when a talk is going on in the Carpenter's Shop the people who are not listening will be quiet so that other people can hear what is said.

A scurry of "sleepers out" in a sudden storm is unavoidable. The noise of the showers is a nuisance but is not complained about, but need the people who bathe after the talk has started talk and laugh quite so loudly? If the sleepers-out have retired early and wish to talk to their neighbours, need such talk be loud enough to drown the words of the speaker inside? If someone must walk across the room, need they plant their heels down quite so heavily? And if latecomers to the talk bring stools, need they scrape them on the ground, sit on them, change their minds and position, and scrape them again before settling down? I could go on with the questions: it is probably only thoughtlessness, but it is extremely selfish and rude to the speaker who is giving her time and talents in the effort to entertain or instruct other people and so help them to pass an hour of darkness pleasantly.

There are many women in the Camp who have had interesting experiences which many of us would like to hear about, but they are not all experienced in public speaking, and they are not likely to be encouraged to offer their services if they know they cannot hope for reasonable silence.

When questions are invited at the close of a talk it would be a help if the questions were audible as well as the answers.

Perhaps one of the Entertainment Committee could announce talks in the supper queue and ask people who are likely to be outside the Carpenter's Shop to please remember the time of the talk, and observe reasonable quietude for that time.

E.A.L.

* * * * *

Entertainment

During the past week, three black-out talks were given to the Camp. The first two held in the Carpenter's shop were by Mrs. Elkins on War Time Cities. Mrs. Elkins' work kept her out of internment until about a fortnight ago and she was interested to tell us about Singapore. Her experiences in Palestine after the last war were a further fascinating part of her talks.

On Monday evening Mrs. Bloom gave an informal lecture on her work in a girls' reformatory. This was held in E Block garden.

At 8.45 p.m. on Wednesday 11 June, Miss Griffith Jones will give a talk on "Experiences, 1911–1918" in the E Block garden if fine, otherwise in the Carpenter's Shop.

Mrs. Dickinson will give a piano recital in the Carpenter's Shop on Friday 12 June at 8.45 p.m.

* * * * *

17 June 1942

Committee Notes

On Sunday 14 June 1942, Lt. Okasaki sent for the Executive Committee from the Men's and Women's Camps. He handed over lists from the Volunteer Camp of men who were enquiring for relatives interned in Changi Gaol, and added that the lists were not yet complete.

On Monday 15 June the Camp Representative and Liaison Officer was approached by the Garrison Command through the interpreter with a view to arranging for the distribution of presents to the ladies who had been sewing badges. (These were badges for military uniforms and the work was compulsory.) She replied that no lady would want a personal present as the badges were being sewn as a Camp duty in view of the order that had been given. We would like to have money for the work as a Camp, as we proposed to give the money to charity. She was then asked to send five ladies from the early list of those who had been sewing to discuss the matter. The following five, Miss Brown, Mrs. Dixon, Mrs. Ferguson, Mrs. de Moubray and Mrs. Taplyn then went to the interview with the interpreter and gave the same answer. No conclusion was reached but they suggested that the two Bishops in Singapore should be contacted with a view to handing over the proceeds. The other sewers whose names were on the list were then collected and informed of the positions. All agreed that no personal presents would be accepted.

The door of the main corridor beyond E Block is now locked by order of the Garrison Command every night at 9.15 p.m. The key is kept by the Camp Representative and Liaison Officer and can be obtained from her in case of emergency.

The flour position is now becoming serious. From 17 June there will be a daily issue of bread of 1½ oz. only. An attempt is being made to buy bread outside but at present permission has not been given for bread to be bought for all camp members.

The Central Finance committee have now granted credit up to $1,000 for penniless people. This fund for essentials will be administered by the Camp Committee. The Camp Committee drew up a list last week of the articles that should be regarded as essentials, but in view of the small amount of the grant it will be necessary to revise the list. The list will be posted as soon as it is drawn up. It was originally arranged that the Camp Representative and Liaison Officer should decide who was eligible for credit grants, but at her suggestion the Camp Committee agreed that, preferably the decisions should be made by the three officers, the Camp Representative and Liaison Officer, and the Camp Superintendent, acting together.

After an inspection last week by the Japanese High Command the Men's Camp were informed that their Camp was not kept clean enough. Instances of people playing cards in passages and dropping cigarette stubs on the ground were mentioned. Our Camp did not receive the same notice, but bridge and mahjong players are often content to drop cigarette ends on the floor and stubs are often found in the main corridor where smoking is not allowed. It would appear that some people still do not realise that all cleaning in this Camp is done by fellow internees and not by paid servants.

Some Changi Cookery Hints

• DO NOT throw away prune-stones without first cracking them for the kernels. These are good alone or make a very palatable addition to the fried savoury rice.

• PINEAPPLE JUICE. Chop the skin of a pineapple small, cover with cold water and bring to the boil over a moderate fire. Boil for about 5 minutes or till you think all the juice is extracted. This makes a very sweet pleasant drink and said to be especially good for the kidneys.

• DO NOT throw away papaya seeds. They taste like mustard besides being very wholesome, and make an excellent flavouring in the daily soup or in a fried savoury rice.

• DO NOT throw away cheese rinds. Fry them, as they are very palatable and also contain all the nourishment of the cheese.

Caution

There seem to be a lot of colds about and a number of people have been admitted to hospital with flu. Take all possible care of yourself. Stay out in the open as much as you can, see that your bedding is aired every day (we know it rains, but use your common sense). Drink plenty of water and as much lime juice as you can get and see that your bowels are kept open. If you feel a cold coming on, take it easy and swallow some aspirins; if you have any quinine, all the better.

The Camp doctors have plenty of work but they are never too busy to advise you if you are worried about your health. The standard of the Camp depends upon each individual.

* * * * *

1 July 1942

Committee Notes

At the General Meeting on Thursday 25 June the present executive officers tendered their resignation. This was done in spite of the fact that a vote of confidence was passed in the present officers, as they felt that the elections had taken place in very early days, and that the members of the Camp had now had time to get to know each other. The elections are now in progress.

At a recent inspection of the Camp 2nd Lt. Takuda stated that all ladies playing mahjong did not stand up when the inspecting party arrived. He has said that if this occurs again he will confiscate all mahjong sets and bridge cards.

Miss Foss, the Camp Superintendent

Who puts two people in a cell
Where really only one should dwell
And makes them clean it out as well?
    The Camp Superintendent.

Who even watches while we eat
One bun, one egg, one piece of meat
While she herself is quite replete?
    The Camp Superintendent.

Who gives an arduous tasks to do
Light fires, sweep floors, flush drains with Sue
Then gives one cigarette too few?
    The Camp Superintendent.

Who will not let us talk to men
Nor chatter loudly after ten
Nor beard Takuda in his den?
    The Camp Superintendent.

When to the court the bins we bear
Who will not let us linger there
But shouts "The High Command is here!"?
    The Camp Superintendent.

Who takes our shoes, controls the shower,
Insists upon the silent hour,
In fact we all are in her power?
    The Camp Superintendent!

                        Anon.

About the Author

Mary Thomas travelled to Singapore in 1939 with her brother Francis, who was returning to his teaching job at St. Andrews School. When war came to Singapore, she chose to stay rather than be evacuated. During internment at Changi Gaol she secretly kept a diary, which is the basis of this book.

After the war, Mary returned to Britain and taught at state secondary schools in Gloucestershire and Essex. She retired in the 1960s and moved to a cottage near Monmouth in south Wales, close to where her brother David lived. Embracing her Celtic roots, Mary studied Welsh and joined Plaid Cymru, the Welsh nationalist party. She became proficient enough in the language to translate medieval Welsh poetry into modern Welsh for the National Library of Wales.

In 1998, failing eyesight made living by herself difficult and Mary, aged 92, moved into residential care. With the radio, audio books and the help of friends who read to her, she kept up with the news and continued to enjoy poetry and other literature. Mary was delighted to learn that In the Shadow of the Rising Sun was to be republished. On 9 February 2009, two months after celebrating her 102nd birthday and just as this book was going into print, she died in her sleep.